# Paper Cuts

pretend there's a way of getting through into it, somehow, Kitty. Let's pretend the glass has got all soft like gauze, so that we can get through. Why, it's

...of mist now. I declare! It'll be easy enough to get through——" She was up on the chim-ney-piece while she said this, though she hardly knew how she got there. And certainly the glass was begin-ning to melt away, just like a bright silvery mist.

In another moment Alice was through the glass, and had jumped lightly down into the Looking-glass room. The very first thing she did was to look

...fire in the fireplace, and she was quite pleased to find that there was a real one, blaz-ing away as brightly as the one she had left behind. "So I shall be as warm here as I was in the old room," thought Alice: "warmer, in fact, because there'll be

# Paper Cuts

## 35 INVENTIVE PROJECTS

Taylor Hagerty

# LARK BOOKS

A Division of Sterling Publishing Co., Inc.
New York / London

**A RED LIPS 4 COURAGE
COMMUNICATIONS, INC. BOOK**

www.redlips4courage.com

**PRESIDENT**
Eileen Cannon Paulin

**DEVELOPMENT DIRECTOR**
Erika Kotite

**DIRECTOR OF EDITORIAL**
Catherine Risling

**EDITOR**
Rebecca Ittner

**ART DIRECTOR**
*the*BookDesigners

**COPY EDITORS**
Christine Allen-Yazzi
Catherine Risling

**PHOTOGRAPHERS**
Rebecca Ittner,
pages 10, 12, 13, 16, 19;
Zac Williams

Library of Congress Cataloging-in-Publication Data

Hagerty, Taylor.
  Paper cuts : 35 inventive projects / Taylor Hagerty. – 1st ed.
    p. cm.
  Includes index.
  ISBN 978-1-60059-512-7 (pb-pbk. : alk. paper)
  1. Paper work. I. Title.
  TT870.H223 2010
  736'.98–dc22

                                    2009022037

10  9  8  7  6  5  4  3  2  1

First Edition

Published by Lark Books, A Division of Sterling Publishing Co., Inc.
387 Park Avenue South, New York, NY 10016

Text © 2010, Taylor Hagerty
Photography © 2010, Red Lips 4 Courage Communications, Inc.
Illustrations © 2010, Red Lips 4 Courage Communications, Inc.

Distributed in Canada by Sterling Publishing,
c/o Canadian Manda Group, 165 Dufferin Street
Toronto, Ontario, Canada M6K 3H6

Distributed in the United Kingdom by GMC Distribution Services,
Castle Place, 166 High Street, Lewes, East Sussex, England BN7 1XU

Distributed in Australia by Capricorn Link (Australia) Pty Ltd.,
P.O. Box 704, Windsor, NSW 2756 Australia

If you have questions or comments about this book, please contact:
Lark Books
67 Broadway
Asheville, NC 28801
828-253-0467

Manufactured in China

ISBN 13: 978-1-60059-512-7

For information about custom editions, special sales, premium and corporate purchases,
please contact Sterling Special Sales Department at 800-805-5489 or specialsales@sterlingpub.com.

# CONTENTS

**8 INTRODUCTION**

**10 CHAPTER 1:** GETTING STARTED

    12 Tools & Materials

    16 Techniques

**20 CHAPTER 2:** LET'S CELEBRATE

    22 Gate-Fold Invitation

    24 Tea Apron

    26 Tea Party Centerpiece

    30 Tea Party Place Cards

    32 Tea Party Placemat

    34 Miniature Papel Picado Flag

    36 Welcome Spring Table Runner

    38 Kirigami Mandala

**40 CHAPTER 3:** DIMENSIONAL DÉCOR

    42 Acorn Luminary

    46 Heron Ornament

    48 Tassel Shelf Liner

    50 Paper Forest

    54 Ginkgo Leaf Lampshade

    56 Falling Leaves Window Valance

    58 Large Flower Ornament

    60 Fairies in the Vines Ornament

    62 Alice Invents Book Sculpture

**64 CHAPTER 4:** SUITABLE FOR FRAMING

    66 The Swan

    68 Never-Too-Late Book Sculpture

    70 Orange Street & Broad Street Gates

    74 The Twins

    76 Dolly

    78 The Beetle's Devotion

    80 Butterfly Grave

82 **CHAPTER 5:** FOR GIVE AND TAKE

84 Kirigami Card

88 Flowers & Butterfly Card

90 Bird of Paradise Ikebana Pop-Up Card

92 Initial Gift Tag

94 Frames & Embellishments

96 Squirrel in the Woods Card & Envelope

98 Feathered Friends Treat Cone

100 The Frog Prince

102 Cowgirl Apron

105 **PATTERNS**

125 **MEET THE DESIGNERS**

128 **INDEX**

# Introduction

ALTHOUGH PAPER CUTTING has a long and storied past, it continues to be a vibrant form of expression. Many of the artists featured in *Paper Cuts* are influenced by its traditions, but have found their own creative voice. Depending on who you ask, it can be called an art or a craft. It is both decorative and functional. It can be a comforting pastime or a lucrative career. Its popularity may rise and fall, but paper cutting is experiencing a revival among artists and crafters of all ages and skill levels.

Available and affordable for everyone, paper cutting requires few materials to get started. Learning the basics is easy—the most important skills are patience and time. Though the simplest patterns can be cut in minutes, some designs can take the advanced paper cutter months to complete. Today's paper cut artists have no fear in pushing the boundaries of this craft.

Paper cuts can now be seen in all areas of pop culture, from haute couture dresses and *Vogue* magazine cover art to museum installations and upscale gallery shows. Its influences can also be seen in décor such as cutout designs on headboards and pillows.

Paper cutting began in China, where artisans cut designs for screens, window coverings, and embroidery patterns. Over the centuries paper cutting was introduced to countries and cultures all over the world, and each developed its own unique designs and styles.

Modern paper cut artists like Cynthia Ferguson and La Donna Welter have taken inspiration from scherenschnitte, which originated in Germany and Switzerland in the 1500s. Ferguson and Welter have pushed this symmetrical style to new heights by infusing their work with contemporary flair, creating unique layered designs.

Janine Maves' designs include elements of wycinanki, a Polish paper cutting art form that employs bright colors and multiple layers of papers that are folded and cut in repeating symmetrical and folk motifs. Maves creates edgy paper cuts using brightly colored papers and then sews them into amazing ornaments and sculptural pieces.

Karin Marlett Choi and Cynthia Emerlye's designs are influenced by kirigami, a blend of origami and paper cutting from Japan. Choi and Emerlye make beautiful, dimensional paper cuts that lend an exciting quality to this age-old style.

Kathleen Trenchard pays homage to the Mexican art of papel picado. Usually made from tissue paper, the designs are cut using a guide and small chisels, or with small scissors. Trenchard works in the traditional style to produce delicate works done with a decidedly modern touch.

In this book you will find everything you need to know to create unique and beautiful paper cut projects designed by some of today's most popular paper cut artists. From layered flowers to intricate centerpieces and unusual book sculptures, their designs are sure to inspire you to pick up your scissors and get cutting.

## Chapter One
# GETTING STARTED

PAPER CUTTING in all its forms is as simple as this: choosing a paper, transferring a design onto the paper, and cutting out the design. The type of paper used to create a paper cut influences how easy or difficult the design is to cut as well as the overall look and feel of the design. Many paper cut artists work with white or off-white paper. White is a great color for beginners since the cuts can easily be seen. Colored and patterned paper can bring depth or a fun feel to a paper cut project.

Ideas for paper cut designs can be found all around you, from books to nature. The modern designs featured in this book are unique and reflect each artist's individual style. As you will read, the artists have found their muse in many things—from celebrations and cultural traditions to fairy tales and flowers. Through paper cutting, they can tell a story, honor a loved one, or decorate a room.

In this chapter you will find information about what tools and materials you need, as well as basic techniques and tips from the experts. Once you read through these pages, and practice the techniques on scrap paper, you will be ready to create your own beautiful paper cuts using the designs in the following chapters.

YOU DON'T NEED a big room or expensive or complicated implements to create beautiful paper cuts. You may even have many of the necessary tools and materials already. Following is a list of basic supplies you will need and tips on how to use them.

### ADHESIVES

*Acid-free tape* is a good choice for adhering paper cuts to backgrounds and other surfaces and will not cause paper to break down over time. Masking tape or linen tape can be used to hold mat board or mounting board to a backing.

*Bookmaker's paste* is a safe choice for working with papers that require a strong hold. Craft glue can also be used.

*Glue sticks* are inexpensive and easily found at office supply stores, craft stores, and grocery markets, and they can be used on most paper cut projects.

*Hot glue guns* are used in framed projects to adhere foamcore and other materials.

*Spray adhesive* is the easiest way to adhere paper cuts to backgrounds such as mat board, mounting board, and thick paper.

## CUTTING TOOLS

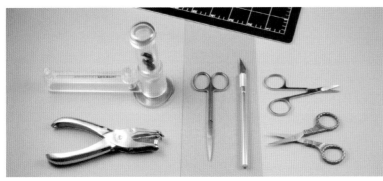

Craft knives and scissors are the tools of choice for paper cutting. Choosing the right size and style is paramount to successful projects. If they are too big, they cannot be maneuvered around tiny details. If they are too small, you risk cutting jagged or crooked lines. Work only with sharp blades—dull or nicked blades can tear or rip paper and can cause you to cut beyond the pattern lines.

*Circular cutting tools* resemble a drawing compass, but have a replaceable blade for cutting circles instead of a pencil for drawing.

*Craft knives* have replaceable blades and are available with metal, plastic, soft, and wood handles. The most common size of blade for paper cutting is #11; unless otherwise noted, use this size when cutting the projects on the following pages.

*Round paper punches* create perfect circles and are available in a wide range of sizes.

*Scissors* with small blades and sharp points are best for paper cutting. Cuticle scissors, embroidery scissors, fine scissors, and manicure scissors are popular choices for paper cutters. They are inexpensive and can easily be found at craft stores, quilting and sewing shops, and online. Iris scissors, also known as surgical scissors, have incredibly sharp blades and are popular among experienced paper cutters.

### CUTTING-EDGE ADVICE

Always use a self-healing cutting mat or other semi-hard surface such as a piece of mat board or non-corrugated cardboard when cutting paper with a craft knife. Doing so will prevent permanent scarring of your tabletops and will help the blades last longer. Working on hard surfaces like glass can cause blades to drag and lift, resulting in uneven cuts and tears in the paper.

Self-healing cutting mats are the surface of choice for the designers featured in this book. Cuts do not damage the mats; their surface remains smooth and unblemished. Consider having a few different sizes on hand.

## PAPER

Just about any paper is suitable for paper cutting. Most paper cutters work with a select few. Each type of paper has its own qualities; some fold easily, while others are sturdy and can withstand a bit of wear and tear. Consider the project as you choose the paper—this will help you make appropriate choices.

Are you going to shape and manipulate the paper for a layered paper cut? If so, you will need a paper that can withstand the work; in this case, watercolor paper would be a great choice. Does your project require a lot of folding? Then choose a paper that can retain a crisp fold, such as letter-weight or scrapbooking paper.

Color and pattern also come into play when deciding which paper to use. For a three-dimensional project, use paper that is the same color on both sides. If you use a patterned paper, make sure that it won't overwhelm the overall design.

Use graphite transfer paper to transfer or trace a design onto the paper that will be cut. Scrap paper is used to protect finished paper cuts during ironing. Backing paper is used on the back of a picture frame to give a finished look to a project. Graphite transfer paper and backing paper can be found at art supply stores and online.

Here are various types of paper to keep on hand:

- **Backing paper**
- **Cardstock**
- **Copy paper**
- **Graphite transfer paper**
- **Letter-weight paper**
- **Parchment paper**
- **Rice paper**
- **Scrapbook paper**
- **Tracing paper**
- **Vellum**
- **Watercolor paper #140**

In addition to the materials and tools listed, add these to your paper cutting arsenal:

- **Bone folder: for scoring folds**
- **Foamcore, mat board, and mounting board: for mounting and framing projects**
- **Framing points, screw eyes, and wire: for framing and hanging projects**
- **Iron: for removing creases and wrinkles from paper**
- **Metal-edged ruler: for cutting straight lines when using a craft knife**
- **Paper clips, staples, and straight pins: for holding projects together during the cutting process**
- **Pencil: for tracing lines**
- **Sewing needle and thread or monofilament: for sewing projects**
- **Soft eraser: for removing pencil lines**

WHETHER YOU USE scissors or a craft knife, there are a few paper cutting techniques you can try. Some paper cut artists move the paper as they cut, not their scissors or craft knife. Others prefer to move their scissors or craft knife instead of the paper. Try both techniques to see which feels most comfortable. You may find that it is easier to cut curvy lines with scissors and straight lines with a craft knife. Thick paper and thin, folded papers are best cut with a craft knife.

## CUTTING & SCORING

*Using a bone folder:* The patterns in this book have two types of lines: dotted lines and straight lines. Dotted lines represent fold lines that you will score using a bone folder. Using the edge of a metal ruler as a guide will help you stay on the dotted line. Straight lines represent cutting lines. Cut along these lines with a craft knife or scissors as instructed in the projects' accompanying instructions.

*Using a craft knife:* Always work so you are pulling the craft knife toward you as you cut, not pushing it away from you. Cut all the vertical lines, then turn the pattern and cut all the horizontal lines. Stop the blade just as it meets the end of a line. If you cut past the line, it is called an overcut. Overcuts can be seen as mistakes in a paper cut project.

### CUTTING-EDGE ADVICE

To copy an image for use as a paper cut pattern, place tracing paper over the picture and trace the image with a pencil. Adhere the tracing paper pattern onto the paper to be cut, or use it along with graphite transfer paper to transfer the image onto the paper.

To cut thin lines with a craft knife, cut from left to right if you are right-handed and right to left if you are left-handed. This will allow you to see the line as you cut, helping you cut the pattern successfully. Use a metal-edged ruler as a guide to help you cut straight lines.

To cut thin lines that cross, start at the crossing point and pull the craft knife toward you.

When working on small interior portions of a pattern, puncture the center of the pattern or cut a small X with the craft knife then complete the cut.

*Using scissors:* Most patterns call for cutting interior portions first. When cutting very small pieces with scissors, puncture the paper with the tip of your scissors, cut to the line, then continue following the cutting line.

Start your cuts with the scissor blades open wide. Don't let the blades close completely as you cut along the lines, as doing so may result in rough or jagged lines.

When working with very thin paper, layer it between the pattern and a piece of copy paper or scrap paper and staple the edges together. This will give added support and make it easier to cut out the pattern.

### ELIMINATING CREASES & FOLDS

Folds, creases, and wrinkles are inherent to the craft of paper cutting. Once you finish cutting and unfolding a paper cut project, use an iron to flatten it. Place clean scrap or tissue paper underneath and on top of the finished paper cut, then gently iron it on a dry setting.

### MOUNTING & FRAMING PAPER CUTS

The most popular background choices are fabric, paper, and mounting or mat board. To make the paper cut pop off the background, use a contrasting color. Center the paper cut on the background then adhere it using adhesive spray, glue, or tape.

---

### CUTTING-EDGE ADVICE

Paper cut artist Barbara Buckingham has developed an easy method to adhere paper cut projects with spray adhesive. She explains, "Using the tip of a craft knife, slowly and carefully lift one bottom corner of the project off the work surface and use your fingertips and thumb to lift the opposite top corner. Gently lift the remainder of the project off the work surface. Ease the project into position on the receiving surface; take your time as you place the project as it can be difficult to reposition some paper cuts."

To successfully use spray adhesive, cover your work surface with newspaper or scrap paper, turn the project facedown on the covered work surface, and then spray the back of the project with adhesive. Make sure your work space is clean before you start the project.

When framing flat paper cuts, press the glass or clear acrylic sheet against the piece to hold the paper cut in place. For dimensional pieces, use a deep shadow box, so as not to damage the paper cut. Consider using a local frame shop to frame the piece if you can't do it.

## PRESERVING & STORING PAPER CUTS

To keep your projects intact, consider using materials to help preserve them. Acid-free products including adhesive spray, glue, and tape will not cause paper to break down over time and are a good choice for adhering paper cuts to backgrounds and other surfaces. UV glass or acrylic sheets will protect framed paper cuts from fading and discoloration.

To store unframed paper cuts, wrap them in newspaper or acid-free tissue paper. Flatten the projects, making sure you don't bend or fold them when wrapping. Place the wrapped pieces between two pieces of mounting or mat board to protect them for long-term storage or mailing.

## USING PATTERNS

The patterns in this book can be used a couple of ways. If you are computer savvy and have access to a scanner and printer, you may wish to scan the patterns into your computer. Then you can enlarge or reduce them as desired and choose the color of ink to use on your printouts. This will give you the freedom to print the patterns directly onto both light- and dark-colored paper and cardstock. Use dark-colored ink on light-colored paper and light- or bright-colored ink on dark-colored paper.

If you don't have access to a scanner, use a copier to copy the patterns onto paper. Depending on the project, you can either copy the pattern directly onto the paper you will be cutting or onto copy paper. The copy paper can then be attached to the paper to be cut, or it can be used along with graphite transfer paper to trace the pattern onto the paper.

*Chapter Two*

# LET'S CELEBRATE

CELEBRATIONS MARK joyous occasions like anniversaries, birthdays, graduations, holidays, and cultural traditions. You may even find that sometimes a special event just may be a small gathering of friends and family, invited to simply enjoy each other's company. Whatever the inspiration, you can make your event memorable with wonderfully handmade paper cut details.

As you plan your special day, decide on a theme for the décor. Are you hosting an afternoon tea party for your best friends, a loved one's birthday, or a get-together for game day? Choose colors that help underscore your chosen theme. Look around for opportunities to create unique elements that will ensure that your fête is a day your guests will long remember. Start with the invitation—this is the first impression guests will have of what you have planned for them, so make it beautiful. An elegant hand-cut paper centerpiece will set the stage, and coordinating elements like placemats, place cards, and table decorations will carry the theme through the entire room.

The projects in this chapter were designed with merry making in mind. Barbara Buckingham created a unique gate-inspired invitation. Cynthia Ferguson designed a beautiful and playful centerpiece and coordinating table decorations in the theme of a favorite childhood storybook. Kathleen Trenchard works in the papel picado tradition and designed a mini flag that is perfect for most any special day. The designs help bring your party to life and honor the most precious things of all: friends and family.

# GATE-FOLD
# INVITATION

Barbara Buckingham

I NSPIRED BY A BEAUTIFUL gate I saw in South Carolina, this card opens from the center, just like the gate. The inside of the card may be handwritten, or you may also consider printing out the information onto cardstock or vellum and attaching it to the inside of the card with glue or brads.

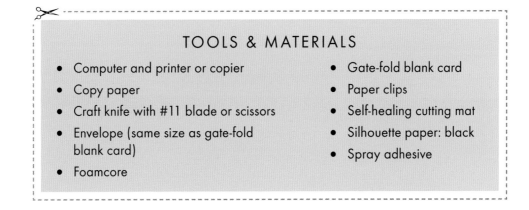

## TOOLS & MATERIALS

- Computer and printer or copier
- Copy paper
- Craft knife with #11 blade or scissors
- Envelope (same size as gate-fold blank card)
- Foamcore
- Gate-fold blank card
- Paper clips
- Self-healing cutting mat
- Silhouette paper: black
- Spray adhesive

## INSTRUCTIONS

1. Copy or print out the Invitation pattern (page 105) onto copy paper. Lay the pattern on the white side of the silhouette paper and adhere using paper clips, making sure that paper and pattern line up.

2. Place the paper on the cutting surface black side down.

3. Start cutting from the interior of the design. *Note:* If you are using a blade, cut in a clockwise direction with your right hand and slowly move the paper counterclockwise with your left hand. If you are left-handed, cut in a counterclockwise direction and move the paper with your right hand in a clockwise direction. The outside edge will be cut going counterclockwise if you are right-handed and clockwise for lefties. This is not as complicated as it sounds. If you are using scissors, cut counterclockwise with your right hand, moving the paper clockwise with your left hand. The outside will be cut in a clockwise direction. Again, the procedure is just the opposite if you are left-handed. The idea is to have the paper move and not the scissors (or blade).

Twisting the blade or scissors can cause you to lose control.

4. After the piece is cut out, prepare the surface that it will be adhered to (in this case, the gate-fold blank card), making sure it is free from dust or dirt.

5. Lay the cutting facedown on a piece of foamcore, and then spray the back of the gate with adhesive.

6. To ready the gate pieces for positioning on the card, pick up the lower right corner of one piece with your left index finger and thumb, lift it off the surface, and then grab the diagonal corner with your right index finger and thumb. Carefully position the lower left corner on one side of the front of the gate-fold card, then lower carefully toward the upper right corner. Repeat for the other side of the gate fold. *Note:* I find this step to be most critical because, once the paper is in position, there is no undoing it.

7. Trim the edges of the cuttings, if needed.

# TEA APRON

## Holly Christian

I LOVE THE FEMININE LINES of this tea apron and have made them for thank-you gifts and party favors. If you want to protect your apron from stains, consider laminating it. Though it won't be as pliable after laminating, it will withstand multiple uses.

## TOOLS & MATERIALS

- Circular paper punch: ¼ inch (0.6 cm)
- Computer and printer or copier
- Copy paper: 11 x 17 inches (27.9 x 43.2 cm)
- Craft knife or scissors
- Glue stick
- Iron with dry setting
- Metal-edged ruler
- Pencil
- Self-healing cutting mat
- Thai soft Unryu paper: white, 23 x 34 inches (58.4 x 86.4 cm)
- Tissue paper: white

## INSTRUCTIONS

*Note:* The finished tea apron is approximately 14 inches (35.6 cm) square with ¾ x 36-inch (1.9 x 91.4 cm) ties.

1. Copy or print out the Tea Apron pattern (page 108) onto copy paper.

2. Iron the Thai soft Unryu paper to flatten it and remove any wrinkles. *Note:* Usually a dry iron will suffice, but if the paper is especially wrinkled, use the lowest steam setting to iron the paper.

3. Cut the Thai soft Unryu paper in half so you have two 17 x 23-inch (43.2 x 58.4 cm) pieces. From these pieces cut one 14-inch (35.6 cm) square, four 2 x 14-inch (5.1 x 35.6 cm) pieces, and one 2 x 23-inch (5.1 x 58.4 cm) piece.

4. Fold the 14-inch (35.6 cm) square piece in half. Place the Tea Apron pattern on the square, lining up the pattern fold line with the fold of the paper.

5. Using the craft knife or scissors, cut the scalloped edge. Using the circular paper punch, create a hole in the center of each scallop. Lay the cut piece open, place a piece of tissue paper over the apron, and iron carefully on a dry setting to flatten. Set the cut apron piece aside.

6. To make the apron ties, glue together the 2-inch (5.1 cm) strips of paper to make one long strip, making sure to overlap the edges a little bit. Fold the long strip in thirds lengthwise and glue down one of the folds.

7. Place the strip horizontally on your work surface with the glued-down flap at the top. Center the cut apron piece faceup on the tie and glue it to the bottom part of the tie.

8. Fold the finished edge of the tie over the apron top and glue in place. Continue folding and gluing the apron ties until you reach the end of the ties. Trim each side to about 36 inches (91.4 cm). Place a piece of tissue paper on top of the finished apron and press with the iron on a dry setting.

# TEA PARTY CENTERPIECE

### Cynthia Ferguson

**W**HEN I WAS ASKED to design a paper cut centerpiece, I looked around for inspiration. Ideas for my paper cuts come from a variety of sources including books (all kinds of books, from storybooks to craft books), artists, and window displays. I also love theme parties and decided to use the opportunity to create a centerpiece for a tea party. What better theme for a tea party than one of my favorite stories, "Alice in Wonderland"?

## TOOLS & MATERIALS

- Computer and printer or copier
- Copy paper
- Craft knife or scissors
- Craft tape
- Self-healing cutting mat
- Thick cardstock or printmaking paper: at least #110

## INSTRUCTIONS

1. Copy or print out Centerpiece A and Centerpiece B patterns (page 106) onto copy paper. In order for the project to be successful, you must use the same percentage when enlarging/printing both patterns.

2. Cut loosely around the outer lines of each pattern, leaving a ½-inch (1.3 cm) edge past the outer lines.

3. Tape each pattern to the cardstock or printmaking paper. *Note:* I used #120 printmaking paper to create this centerpiece.

4. Cut out one piece at a time, cutting out the inside portions first. This will ensure that the pattern stays adhered to your project as you work.

5. When you have cut out all the inside pieces, cut the outer edge of the pattern.

6. Cut the two notches in the center of both pieces.

7. Assemble the two pieces together, referencing the finished project photograph as needed.

# TEA PARTY PLACE CARDS

Cynthia Ferguson

I DESIGNED THESE CHARMING place cards to be used with the Tea Party Centerpiece. Once you are finished cutting the place cards, add a guest's name to each one. If you don't want to write names by hand, consider stamping them or printing them onto clear labels that can be adhered to the front of the place cards.

## TOOLS & MATERIALS

- Bone folder
- Computer and printer or copier
- Copy paper
- Craft knife or scissors
- Craft tape
- Self-healing cutting mat
- Thick cardstock or printmaking paper: at least #110

## INSTRUCTIONS

1. Copy or print out the Place Cards patterns (page 107) onto copy paper.

2. Cut loosely around the outer lines of each pattern, leaving a ½-inch (1.3 cm) edge past the outer lines.

3. Tape the patterns to the cardstock or printmaking paper. *Note:* I used #120 printmaking paper to create these place cards. Using the bone folder, score the dotted lines.

4. Cut out one place card at a time, cutting out the inside portions first. This will ensure that the patterns stay adhered to your project as you work. *Note:* Make sure when cutting the outlines for the teacups or kettle that you cut only those lines; if you extend beyond the lines, the overcuts will be noticeable.

5. When you have cut out all the inside pieces, cut the outer edges of the patterns.

6. Fold as shown on patterns, add your guest's name, and display.

# TEA PARTY PLACEMAT

Cynthia Ferguson

THIS INTRICATE PLACEMAT was designed to be used with the Tea Party Centerpiece and Tea Party Place Cards. I chose teapots to complement the tea party theme. To protect the surface of the placemat and preserve it for future use, consider laminating the piece.

## TOOLS & MATERIALS

- Bone folder
- Computer and printer or copier
- Copy paper
- Craft knife or scissors
- Paper tape
- Pencil
- Self-healing cutting mat
- Watercolor paper: #140

## INSTRUCTIONS

1. Copy or print out the Tea Party Placemat pattern (page 108) onto copy paper.

2. Draw a large perpendicular X on the watercolor paper.

3. Match the dotted lines of the pattern with the inside portion of the upper left section of the X.

4. Tape the pattern to the watercolor paper. Score the papers along the dotted lines; do not cut the dotted lines.

5. Cut out the gray areas on the pattern first, and then cut the outside edges.

6. Remove the pattern and flip it over so it matches up with right side of the X.

7. Repeat steps 4-6 to finish cutting the placemat.

# MINIATURE PAPEL PICADO FLAG

Kathleen Trenchard

THESE LITTLE FLAGS ARE a quick way to add some fun to any celebration. I often use them to dress up a room for a special occasion. Consider creating individual arrangements using multiple flags and then putting one at each guest's place setting.

## TOOLS & MATERIALS

- Computer and printer or copier
- Copy paper
- Glue stick
- Paper clips or stapler
- Ruler
- Scissors
- Tissue paper: assorted colors
- Wooden skewers: about 12 inches (30.5 cm) long

## INSTRUCTIONS

1. Copy or print out the Flag pattern (page 105) onto copy paper. Using paper clips or a stapler, attach the pattern to the top of a stack of three sheets of colored tissue paper. Be careful to place paper clips or staples only on the black areas of the pattern. *Note:* I recommend using 4 x 6-inch (10.2 x 15.2 cm) pieces of tissue paper—this will make it easy to cut out the pattern.

2. Cut out all of the black shapes, starting in the center and working outward. Cut the border of the pattern, making sure all layers are flat.

3. To create the fringe crown for the flag using scraps of tissue paper, cut three 2 x 3-inch (5.1 x 7.6 cm) rectangles of different colors. Layer the rectangles and cut thin vertical strips about half way down the 3-inch (7.6 cm) side. You should have five or six vertical cuts.

4. Apply glue to the uncut area of each rectangle, and then glue the uncut ends together. Apply glue to one uncut side and wrap the edge around the top of a skewer so the fringe is on top.

5. Apply glue to the extension side of a flag, as marked on the pattern, and wrap it tightly around the skewer, covering the uncut edge of the fringe crown.

# WELCOME SPRING
# TABLE RUNNER

Holly Christian

**T**HIS PRETTY TABLE RUNNER will bring a touch of elegance to any room or celebration. When crafted with pale green paper, as seen here, it is perfect for a spring or summer get-together. Feel free to create yours in any color. I made this runner using a heavy-weight, durable paper so it will hold up well for many uses.

## TOOLS & MATERIALS

- Computer and printer or copier
- Copy paper
- Craft knife
- Glue stick
- Iron with dry setting
- Large paper clips (5-6)
- Pencil
- Pointed tweezers
- Scissors
- Self-healing cutting mat
- Thai reversible Unryu paper
- Tissue paper: white

## INSTRUCTIONS

*Note*: Thai reversible Unryu paper is sold in 24 x 35-inch (61.0 x 88.9 cm) sheets. One sheet will make two 11 x 35-inch (27.9 x 88.9 cm) table runners.

1. Copy or print out the Table Runner and Bird patterns (page 109) onto copy paper.

2. Cut the Thai reversible Unryu paper in half lengthwise. Set one piece aside. Fold the remaining piece of paper in quarters by first folding the paper in half lengthwise and then in half again the other direction.

3. Place the pattern on top of the paper, lining up the pattern fold lines with the folds of the paper. Place large paper clips along the fold lines to hold the pattern and paper in place.

4. Cut the edges of the table runner with scissors and the interior portions using the craft knife. *Note:* When folded, this paper is thick so you may need to go over the interior cuts a couple of times.

5. Unfold the paper so only the lengthwise fold remains. Using the bird pattern, cut out the bird that falls on the vertical fold.

6. Open the runner and gently blow or shake out all of the loose bits of paper. Using the pointed tweezers, remove any stubborn pieces of cut paper. Look carefully over your cut piece and clean up any cuts that aren't complete.

7. Cover the runner with tissue paper and iron on a dry setting so the runner will lay flat.

# KIRIGAMI MANDALA

## Cynthia Emerlye

**M**ANDALAS ARE COMPLEX CIRCULAR designs that, when looked at, can have a calming and expanding effect on the mind. Traditionally, they represent the universe and are used as an aid in meditation. In addition to matting and framing finished mandalas, I also enjoy hanging them as decorative accents.

## TOOLS & MATERIALS

- Circular paper punches: 1/16 inch (0.15 cm), 1/8 inch (0.3 cm), 1/4 inch (0.6 cm)
- Computer and printer or copier
- Copy paper
- Craft knife
- Heavyweight scrap paper
- Iron with dry setting
- Parchment paper: 8 x 10 inches (20.3 x 25.4 cm)
- Pencil
- Scissors
- Soft eraser
- Tracing paper

## INSTRUCTIONS

1. Copy or print out the Mandala pattern (page 105) onto copy paper.

2. Cut the parchment paper into a square between 8 and 10 inches (20.3 to 25.4 cm) (Fig. 1). Fold the square diagonally from the top left corner. You now have a triangle (Fig. 2).

3. Fold the paper diagonally again, outer corner to outer corner. You now have a smaller triangle (Fig. 3).

4. Holding the triangular paper at its apex (the point where all of the folds come together), you'll see that one side of the triangle is shorter than the other. Draw an arc from the short side to the long side so that each side is the same length. Cut along the line to trim the excess paper (Fig. 4). Your triangle should now look like an ice cream cone (Fig. 5).

5. Position the tracing paper and Mandala pattern on top of the triangle and trace the design. Make sure that no lines meet side to side.

6. Cut out the design, and then carefully erase any remaining tracing lines. Open the triangle to reveal the finished mandala.

7. Place the mandala between two sheets of heavyweight paper and iron on a dry setting to remove any creases. Your mandala is now ready for display.

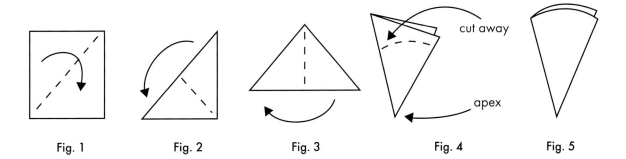

cut away

apex

Fig. 1    Fig. 2    Fig. 3    Fig. 4    Fig. 5

*Chapter Three*

# DIMENSIONAL DÉCOR

DECORATING YOUR HOME with items created with your own hands allows you to customize a wide range of design elements. If you have a difficult time finding just the right lampshade or window treatment, a unique paper cut version will solve your problem in a flash. Embellishing a room becomes a more exciting and rewarding experience when you can step back and look at the beauty you have created.

Small hanging ornaments add a dash of fun and whimsy to windows. They can also be hung from lamp pulls, plants, shelves, and door knobs. Dress up glass-front cabinets with a pretty paper cut shelf liner. Add a dramatic touch to a table top with a unique paper sculpture. Though it may seem like a daunting endeavor, making three-dimensional decorative items is fun and easy.

The projects in this chapter offer something for everyone. Karin Marlett Choi created a beautiful luminary, a lampshade, and a window valance. Janine Maves made an incredible paper forest, perfect for display on a tabletop or bookshelf. Jennifer Khoshbin repurposed an old book by turning it into a unique book sculpture. Use the patterns in this chapter with the paper colors of your choice and create original décor for your home.

# ACORN LUMINARY

Karin Marlett Choi

**M**ANY OF MY PAPER CUT designs are inspired by nature. This tabletop luminary is cut with an oak branch motif and glows with the warmth of autumn. It is both functional and a decorative conversation piece—especially when you tell your guests you made it yourself.

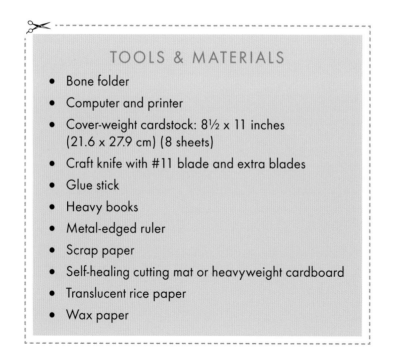

## TOOLS & MATERIALS

- Bone folder
- Computer and printer
- Cover-weight cardstock: 8½ x 11 inches (21.6 x 27.9 cm) (8 sheets)
- Craft knife with #11 blade and extra blades
- Glue stick
- Heavy books
- Metal-edged ruler
- Scrap paper
- Self-healing cutting mat or heavyweight cardboard
- Translucent rice paper
- Wax paper

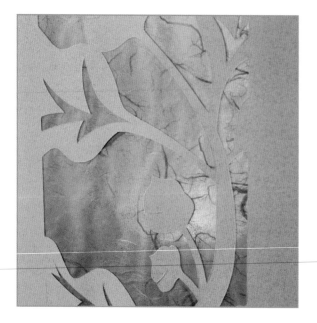

## INSTRUCTIONS

1. Copy or print out the Acorn Luminary pattern (page 109) onto cardstock. Copy two patterns facing one direction and two facing the opposite direction.

2. Using the bone folder, score the cardstock pattern along the vertical and horizontal dotted lines. With the back side of the pattern toward you, fold along the score lines and crease each fold sharply toward the back of the work using the bone folder, creating three tabs. Open cardstock flat again.

3. Using the craft knife, cut out the background shapes of the design. As you are cutting, turn the paper so you are always moving the craft knife toward you.

4. Repeat steps 1 through 3 for the remaining three panels.

5. Cut four pieces of 5¾ x 9¾-inch (14.6 x 24.8 cm) translucent rice paper.

6. Copy or print out the Frames pattern (page 109) onto the remaining four sheets of cardstock; cut out the frames.

7. Working with one sheet of cardstock at a time, spread a thin, even layer of glue on the back side of the border around the oak branch design, avoiding the tabs. Lay the cut rice paper pieces on the glue; put a clean piece of scrap paper over the work and smooth the rice paper flat using the bone folder. *Note:* This creates the shade effect that allows the light to softly shine through.

8. Repeat step 7 with the remaining three panels.

9. Lay all of the panels out side by side with wrong sides facing up and the vertical tabs to your right. (Think of them as panels 1 to 4, from left to right.) Arrange the panels so the design alternates—acorns pointing right, then left, and so on. Working from left to right, fold the vertical tab of the first panel up so the opposite side is facing you. Place a clean piece of scrap paper under the tab and over the rest of the panel to protect it, and then spread a thin layer of glue or paste on the tab. Place the glued tab

CUTTING-EDGE ADVICE

Though the instructions for this project call for translucent rice paper for the background of the panels, you can use any type of translucent paper. I would advise that you steer away from vellum, though, as it can be difficult to glue.

To light the panels, use a small lamp or candle. If you use a candle, be sure to place it in a votive holder to prevent any fire danger. Never leave a burning candle unattended.

onto the left-hand border (one without the tab attached) of the next panel to the right. Be sure to line up the panels using the horizontal score lines as guides. You may also want to flip the joined panels over to be sure the edge of each panel lines up evenly with the folded edge of the tab. Flip the panel back over so the wrong sides are facing up and bond the two panels together using the bone folder. Repeat the same procedure to adhere the two bonded panels with the next panels to the right until all panels are glued together in a line.

10. With the four joined panels wrong side facing up, spread a thin layer of glue on the tabs at the top and bottom of panels 2, 3, and 4. Fold in and glue down. *Note:* This provides stability and helps maintain the bond of the vertical tabs. Do not complete this step on panel 1 yet.

11. Spread a thin layer of glue onto the wrong side of one of the frames made in steps 7 and 8. Center it over the wrong side of panel 2 and glue down over the tabs, using the bone folder to bond the glue. Repeat for panels 3 and 4.

*Note:* This gives the frame of the panels a more finished look and added strength.

12. Spread a thin layer of glue on the final tab on the ends of panel 4 as you did on the other three panels. Place the left-hand border of panel 1 on the glued tab of panel 4, creating a continuous loop of panels. Line up the edges and bond the panels using the bone folder. Finish the panel by gluing the remaining tabs at the top and bottom of panel 1 in toward the inside of the shade. Work carefully, as the piece is no longer flat and you are working inside the shade. Glue the remaining frame over the tabs of panel 1 inside the shade.

13. Fold the shade flat. Place a sheet of wax paper inside the shade and on both sides of the outside. Place a couple of heavy books on top and allow the glue to dry. *Note:* The wax paper will prevent any stray glue or paste from sticking where it shouldn't.

14. Once dry, open the shade. It is now ready to display.

# HERON ORNAMENT

### Janine Maves

I N   P O L A N D ,   P A P E R   C U T T I N G   is often derived from the stenciling found across the ceiling beams in houses; the shapes are often birds. This North Carolina heron is my homage to the birds of Poland. Though the ornament can be cut with scissors, it is best to use a very sharp craft knife so the edges will be much more defined.

## TOOLS & MATERIALS

- Computer and printer or copier
- Copy paper
- Craft knife with #9 blade
- Crisp paper or vellum: white
- Pencil
- Ruler
- Scissors
- Self-healing cutting mat
- Sewing needle
- Soft eraser
- Thread or monofilament: white

## INSTRUCTIONS

*Note:* Crisp white paper works best for a beginner, but you can also use vellum or white-on-white decorative paper.

1. Copy or print out the Heron pattern (page 110) onto copy paper. Cut around the outside edges of the pattern, leaving a ½-inch (1.3 cm) border beyond the lines.

2. Cut two 3½-inch (8.9 cm) squares of paper and fold them in half, using your finger or a ruler to make a sharp crease. Open one of the pieces and place the Heron pattern on top of it. Trace around the pattern lightly with a pencil. Remove the pattern.

3. Fit one creased piece of paper into the other and cut the outside edges only. Take the two pieces of paper apart and make the smaller cuts. Put the second folded piece inside the first and lightly trace the smallest cuts, then cut those, too. You now have two identical herons. Gently erase the penciled tracing lines.

4. Open the two cut pieces of paper and then align the outward creases of the pieces.

5. Using the sewing needle, make small holes down the center crease about ¼ inch (0.6 cm) apart. Using the thread or monofilament, stitch the heron's feet together through one hole. Don't try to knot the end of the thread; instead, pull it through the hole twice, leaving a 2- to 3-inch (5.1 to 7.6 cm) tail of thread at the end. Use this end and the still-threaded needle to tie a double knot, and then continue to sew up the heron's body.

6. Once you've stitched the beak, catch the thread on your finger to form a loop. Run the needle through the beak hole once more and tie a knot using the loop as one string and the still-threaded needle as the other.

7. Clip the thread ends at the top and bottom and fold the piece open both ways to make the four herons' beaks meet at 90-degree angles. The piece is ready to hang.

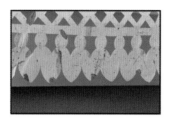

# TASSEL SHELF LINER

Kathleen Trenchard

AN IMPORTANT INGREDIENT in the ambiance and charm of Mexico is the display of merchandise. From inventive and alluring arrangements of fruit on a corner stand to elaborate candy displays, everything is designed with panache. Often these displays are accented with paper elements like this shelf liner. I have created these shelf liners as gifts for housewarmings, weddings, and holiday celebrations.

## TOOLS & MATERIALS

- Computer and printer or copier
- Copy paper
- Double-sided tape
- Iron with dry setting
- Paper clips
- Paper glue
- Rice paper or wrapping paper (24 x 36 inches [61.0 x 91.4 cm])
- Scissors or craft knife
- Self-healing cutting mat

## INSTRUCTIONS

1. Cut the 24 x 36-inch (61.0 x 91.4 cm) piece of paper lengthwise. *Note:* You can cut the shelf liner as deep or as shallow as needed; adjust measurements as necessary.

2. Glue one 12-inch (30.5 cm) wide side of each piece together to create an approximately 12 x 72-inch (30.5 x 182.9 cm) long sheet.

3. Copy or print out the Shelf Liner pattern (page 110) onto copy paper. Line up the pattern lengthwise at one end of the paper. Fold and crease the sheet, fan-style, aligning the pattern with the folds. If there is extra paper on the end after folding, either cut it off or fold it once more.

4. Attach paper clips to the folded sides and the top to secure the pattern to the folded paper. Cut out all of the black areas.

5. Remove the paper clips and pattern. Unfold the paper and iron on a dry setting to remove creases, if desired.

6. Place the cut paper liner on a shelf and fold so the cut area hangs over the edge. Trim the sides as needed. Secure the liner to the shelf with double-sided tape.

# PAPER FOREST

Janine Maves

THROUGH A BEAUTIFUL FORM of theater, Indonesians tell stories using intricately cut paper puppets behind a screen. The shapes are backlit and very dramatic. I thought that making a forest from different types of papers using Indonesian techniques would pay tribute to this art. This intricate paper forest would make a lovely holiday centerpiece or mantel decoration. It also can be displayed on a shelf to add visual interest to any room. I made these trees in shades of white and gold, though they can be made in any color.

## TOOLS & MATERIALS

- Computer and printer or copier
- Copy paper
- Craft knife with #9 blade
- Medium-weight paper: gold, plain white, white vellum, or white-on-white patterned
- Pencil
- Scissors
- Self-healing cutting mat
- Sewing needle
- Soft eraser
- Thread or monofilament: white
- Tracing paper

## INSTRUCTIONS

1. Copy or print out the Forest A-F patterns (page 111) onto copy paper. *Note:* To add visual interest to your paper forest, reduce or enlarge the size of the patterns to vary the size of the trees.

2. Cut one piece of tracing paper roughly the size of each pattern.

3. For each tree, cut two rectangles of medium-weight paper the height of the pattern by twice the width of the pattern. Fold the rectangles in half and place a corresponding size of tracing paper on top. Place the fold on the center line of the pattern. Lightly trace the pattern onto the paper.

4. Working on one pattern at a time, use scissors to carefully cut out the outer shape. Next, cut out the interior shape. *Note:* For large interior shapes, cut an X in the negative (dark) areas and use these cuts to maneuver around the traced shapes without bending the paper.

5. Using a craft knife, cut out any small interior shapes. Using a new blade will make interior cuts much easier to complete. You will end up with two matching pairs of the same tree. Keep the pairs together after they are cut; you will stitch them together to create the standing trees for the forest.

6. Gently erase the penciled lines left from tracing the shapes, working toward the cut edge. Make sure to hold the paper firmly on the cutting mat to prevent tears and unwanted bends.

7. Working one pair at a time, stitch the trees together. Using the needle, make small holes down the center crease, about ¼ inch (0.6 cm) apart. Stitch the center creases together with the thread or monofilament, knot the thread, and then trim the ends. *Note:* For the gold Japanese-style tree, stitch the roots together, knot and trim the threads, and then repeat at the top of the tree.

8. Carefully press the sewn seam with your fingers so the two halves open fully and meet at the center axis at a 90-degree angle. *Note:* The right angles and flat bottom of the trees will enable them to stand upright. You may want to cut out three of the moons so there is only one moon in your forest.

# GINKGO LEAF LAMPSHADE

Karin Marlett Choi

SPRUCE UP AN OLD LAMP with this Ginkgo Leaf Lamp-shade. I chose papers that look gorgeous together when the light is on or off. When choosing papers to use in this project, hold a cream paper over a metallic paper and then position them in front of a light source to see if you can see the texture of the bottom paper through the top paper. If you can, you have great papers to make a lovely shade.

## TOOLS & MATERIALS

- Bone folder
- Computer and printer or copier
- Copy paper
- Craft knife with #11 blade and extra blades
- Glue stick
- Lampshade with smooth paper or plastic liner
- Medium-weight mulberry paper: semi opaque, cream
- Metal-edged ruler
- Pencil
- Scissors
- Scrap paper
- Self-healing cutting mat
- Translucent paper: metallic rayon fiber, gold

## INSTRUCTIONS

1. Place the lampshade on the cream mulberry paper. Align the seam of the shade with the edge of the paper. Trace the shape of the shade at the top and bottom as you slowly roll it across the paper.

2. Cut out the shade shape, leaving a ½-inch (1.3 cm) border outside the drawn lines at the top and bottom so the paper is bigger than the lampshade. Use the cut piece of cream mulberry paper as a pattern to cut the same shape from the gold translucent paper.

3. Apply a thin layer of glue to the lampshade frame. Line up the gold translucent paper so the seam falls in the same place as the seam on the frame liner. *Note:* This will help you keep the paper straight as well. Smooth out the paper as you go to avoid bumps and creases.

4. Trim the excess paper from the edges of the lampshade using scissors.

5. Copy or print out the Ginkgo Leaf patterns (page 110) onto copy paper and cut out the shapes. Using the pencil, trace the ginkgo leaf shapes in a random order onto the cream mulberry paper. Using the craft knife, cut out the ginkgo shapes.

6. Apply a thin layer of glue to the backside of the cream mulberry paper, and then line up the paper so that the seam falls in the same place as the seam on the frame liner and the gold translucent paper. Using the bone folder on the inside of the shade against your work surface, burnish the seam to strengthen the bond. You may also need to encourage the edges of the cutouts to stick to the shade in the same manner with your bone folder.

7. Trim the excess paper from the bottom of the lampshade with scissors.

8. Cut vertical slits in the paper that extends beyond the top of the frame, making sure the slits end slightly above the top of the shade. Glue these small strips to the inside of the frame. Allow glue to dry.

9. Place the lampshade on a lamp base and enjoy.

# FALLING LEAVES
# WINDOW VALANCE

Karin Marlett Choi

THE BEAUTIFUL CUTOUTS on this valance not only create an elegant touch for any window, they also let light in with dramatic effect. I created this pattern so it can easily be altered to fit any window width. Depending on the width of your window and your preference for the tightness of the pleats, you'll need between six and ten panels or more.

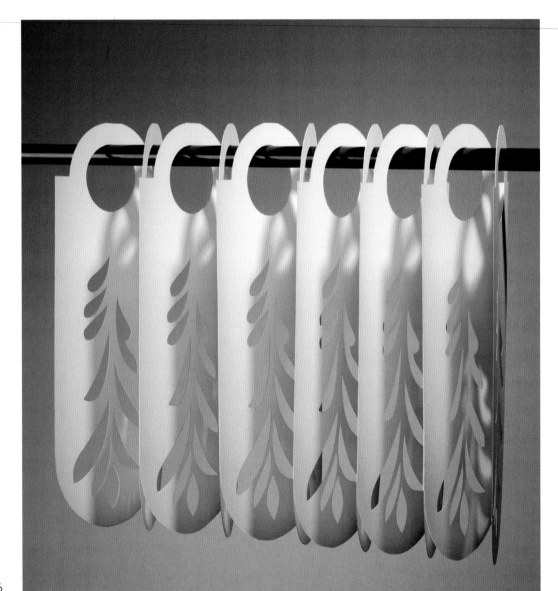

## TOOLS & MATERIALS

- Bone folder
- Circle cutter or 1¾-inch (4.4 cm) round craft punch
- Computer and printer or copier
- Cover-weight cardstock: cream, 8½ x 11 inches (21.6 x 27.9 cm) (6-10 sheets)
- Craft knife with #11 blade and extra blades
- Curtain rod
- Glue stick
- Heavy books
- Scissors
- Scrap paper
- Self-healing cutting mat

## INSTRUCTIONS

1. Copy or print out the Valance pattern (page 112) onto cream cardstock.

2. Place the cardstock pattern on the cutting mat. Using the bone folder, score the cardstock pattern along the vertical dotted lines. With the backside of the cardstock pattern toward you, fold from left to right along the score line, using the bone folder to crease each fold sharply. Next, fold the narrow tab toward the front side of the work. The folds should be going in opposite directions, accordion-style. Open the sheet flat.

3. Using the scissors or craft knife, cut out the outline of the valance panel. Using the craft knife, cut out the leaf shapes. *Note:* As you are cutting, turn the paper so you are always drawing the knife toward you. Cut out the circle using the circle cutter or craft punch.

4. Re-fold the centerfold so the back of each panel is folded on the inside, and then fold the tab toward the front of the panel as in step 2.

5. Repeat steps 1-4 on each sheet of cardstock.

6. Spread a thin, even layer of glue on the front side of the tab and stick it to the back of the next panel. Slide the panel onto the glued tab, lining it up with the straight edge at the top of the panel and butting the long edge up against the crease to make sure it is lined up straight.

7. Working from the center outward, eliminate air bubbles and press the two surfaces together using the bone folder, making the glue bond strong. *Note:* Place a clean piece of scrap paper between the work and the bone folder to prevent distorting.

8. Repeat until all panels are glued together. Once you've made the valance the length you want, cut the last tab off the last panel. The valance will fold back and forth on itself in an accordion fashion. Place the folded valance under a couple of heavy books and allow the glue to dry.

9. Thread a curtain rod through the round holes in the valance and hang. Stretch the valance to cover the width of your window.

# LARGE FLOWER ORNAMENT

Janine Maves

T HIS COMPLICATED FLOWER shape was inspired by pictures I saw of some amazing kirigami pieces. You can add a fun design element to any room by hanging this flower ornament from a tall lamp, ceiling fan, shelf, banister, or window. To make a grouping of flowers, print out multiple patterns in varying sizes. Just remember to adjust the length of thread or monofilament for each size. Make sure the paper you choose for this project is the same color on both sides.

## TOOLS & MATERIALS

- Beads to hang from bottom of ornament (1–4)
- Bone folder
- Colored or patterned paper of your choice
- Computer and printer or copier
- Copy paper
- Craft knife with #9 blade
- Pencil
- Ruler
- Scissors
- Self-healing cutting mat
- Sewing needle
- Soft eraser
- Thread to match the paper or monofilament

## INSTRUCTIONS

1. Copy or print out the Large Flower and Bud patterns (page 113) onto copy paper and cut out the shapes.

2. Cut two 6¾ x 5¼-inch (17.1 x 13.3 cm) rectangles of paper, and then fold each piece in half widthwise. Using the bone folder, make a sharp crease. Nest one rectangle inside the other and lay the Large Flower pattern on top of the outer rectangle. Using a pencil, lightly trace the pattern onto the rectangle.

3. Using scissors, cut the outer lines of the pattern. Using the craft knife, cut the interior lines of the pattern. You now have two identical pairs of flowers. Select the largest piece of leftover paper to create the flower bud. Lay the Bud pattern on top of the paper, trace the shape, and then cut it out. Repeat for second flower bud shape.

4. Firmly hold the cut pieces down on a flat surface and erase the traced lines, working from the inside out toward the edge.

5. Open the two cut large flower shapes and place the outward creases of the pieces together. Using the needle, make small holes along the center crease about ¼ inch (0.6 cm) apart. Repeat with the bud shapes.

6. Using the needle and thread or monofilament, pass the needle through the bead twice, leaving an 8- to 9-inch (20.3 to 22.9 cm) tail of thread on the end. Tie a double knot around the bead with the still-threaded needle. *Note:* If you use more than one bead, run the thread through the top bead twice to keep it from sliding up and down.

7. Insert the needle in the lowest hole on the large flower shape's crease; sew through the next hole, and then sew through the first hole again. Adjust the bead(s) so it hangs about 1 inch (2.5 cm) below the flower. Secure the thread by sewing through the bottom hole twice. Continue sewing up along the seam, passing through the top hole twice to secure the thread.

8. Leave a 1-inch (2.5 cm) blank space of thread between the top of the large flower and the bud. Sew through the seams of the bud, passing through the top hole twice to secure the thread.

9. Once you've made the last stitch, catch the thread on your finger to form a loop. Run the needle through the top hole once more and tie a knot using the loop as one string and the still-threaded needle as the other. Trim the thread.

10. Fold both the large flower and bud open both ways to make the four sprays of flowers meet at 90-degree angles at the center axis. Your ornament is ready to hang.

# FAIRIES IN THE VINES ORNAMENT

Janine Maves

I'VE ALWAYS LOVED the way architects use sculpted human bodies as structural support. This ornament features a female figure that was inspired by the corner of an Indian temple. It struck me that the figure would make a dramatic paper cutting so I used that shape to create my Fairies in the Vines Ornament. The ornament is a perfect decoration for any spring or summer party, or it can cheer up a little girl's bedroom in a flash. Use double-sided paper for this project.

## TOOLS & MATERIALS

- Beads (1–2)
- Bone folder
- Colored or printed paper of your choice
- Computer and printer or copier
- Copy paper
- Craft knife with #9 blade
- Pencil
- Ruler
- Scissors
- Self-healing cutting mat
- Sewing needle
- Soft eraser
- Thread to match the paper or monofilament

## INSTRUCTIONS

1. Print out or copy the Fairies pattern (page 113) onto copy paper and cut out the shapes.

2. Cut two 4¼ x 4½-inch (10.8 x 11.4 cm) rectangles from the color or printed paper and fold each one in half widthwise. Using the bone folder, make a sharp crease.

3. Nest one rectangle inside the other, and then place the cut pattern on the top rectangle. Trace the pattern onto the outer rectangle. Cut the outside edges only, and then remove the inner shape. You will now work on one shape at a time.

4. Using the craft knife, cut out the inner shapes of the once-outer rectangle. Place the cut ornament (still folded in half) on top of the remaining rectangle. Trace the cut inner shapes with the pencil, and then cut out the shapes with the craft knife. You now have two identical pairs of fairies.

5. Hold the cut pieces firmly against your work surface and carefully erase the traced lines, working from the inside out toward the edges.

6. Open the cut pieces and place the outward creases together. Using the needle, make small holes down the center of the crease, ¼ inch (0.6 cm) apart.

7. Using the needle and thread or monofilament, pass the needle through the bead twice, leaving a 6- to 7-inch (15.2 to 17.8 cm) tail of thread on the end. Tie a double knot around the bead with the still-threaded needle. *Note:* If you use more than one bead, run the thread through the top bead twice to keep it from sliding up and down.

8. Insert the needle in the lowest hole on the crease, sew through the next hole, then sew through the first hole again. Adjust the bead(s) so they hang about 1 inch (2.5 cm) below the flower. Secure the thread by sewing through the bottom hole twice. Continue sewing up along the seam, passing through the top hole twice to secure the thread.

9. Once you've made the last stitch, catch the thread on your finger to form a loop. Thread the needle through the top hole once more and tie a knot using the loop as one string and the still-threaded needle as the other. Trim the ends of the thread.

10. Fold the piece open both ways to make the four fairies meet at 90-degree angles at the center axis. Your ornament is now ready to hang.

# A L I C E   I N V E N T S
# B O O K   S C U L P T U R E

Jennifer Khoshbin

THIS PROJECT IS a great way to recycle and redefine the beauty of a vintage book. I have great luck finding inexpensive books at thrift stores and used book stores. The emphasis of this project is on the beauty of old illustrations, so make sure you select a book with illustrations that you admire and that are easy to cut out. Also, the book pages need to be thick so the illustrations will stand up when cut and bent.

## TOOLS & MATERIALS

- Cardboard or self-healing cutting mat
- Circular paper cutting tool
- Craft knife
- Glue stick
- Old book

## INSTRUCTIONS

1. Place the cardboard or self-healing cutting mat under the first page of the book. Using the craft knife, cut out the illustration, leaving the bottom section intact so that it stands up when folded, referring to the project photograph as needed.

2. With cardboard or cutting mat still in place, cut away the first circle with the circular cutting tool. Remove the cardboard or cutting mat and place it under the second page of the book; reduce the circle size just a touch, then cut and remove the next circle. Continue cutting smaller and smaller circles until the book has been carved out to its smallest circle.

3. Choose a meaningful word from the book's pages. Using the craft knife, cut out the word. Using the glue stick, adhere the word faceup on the first uncut page at the bottom of the circle. *Note:* Be sure to center the word so it can be read through the smallest cut circle.

4. Bend the cutout silhouettes so they stand up. The book sculpture is ready for display.

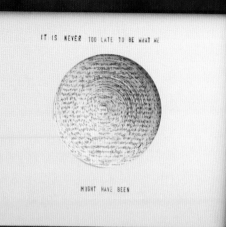

IT IS NEVER TOO LATE TO BE WHAT WE

MIGHT HAVE BEEN

Philip Simmons Gate on Orange Street
Charleston, SC
hand cut paper
Barbara Buckingham 2008

*Chapter Four*

# SUITABLE
# FOR FRAMING

ANY PEOPLE ENVISION old-fashioned framed pieces when they think of paper cutting. The framed paper cuts made today, however, are far from old-fashioned. Exciting new patterns, interesting materials, and fun framing ideas make paper cuts relevant to modern design, giving them a place in any home.

Instead of traditional intricate patterns of people, baskets, and fauna, you will find ballerinas with graceful curves and layered flowers that seem real enough to touch. Now, depth and dimension are often part of framed paper cuts, imparting a new sophistication. Instead of looking at something, you are looking into something. Even flat paper cuts are more whimsical and fresh.

In this chapter you will find framed projects in a wide variety of styles. Tina Tarnoff created an elegant layered dancer. Barbara Buckingham made two gates that are amazingly accurate replicas of those she found in South Carolina. La Donna Welter constructed dimensional life-like flowers. Jennifer Khoshbin's framed altered book is something to behold.

Look around your living space; do you need to liven things up? Give your walls a fresh, new look with one of the paper cut projects on the following pages.

# THE SWAN

## Tina Tarnoff

THIS PROJECT IS SOMEWHAT difficult, but I found the final result very rewarding. The simplicity and clean lines of the design accentuate the elegance and movement of the dancer. Create this piece as a gift or to decorate your walls.

## TOOLS & MATERIALS

- Cardstock: black, 8½ x 11 inches (21.6 x 27.9 cm) (2 sheets); parchment (1 sheet)
- Computer and printer or copier
- Craft knife
- Glue pen
- Mounting board: black, 11 x 14 inches (27.9 x 35.6 cm)
- Self-healing cutting mat
- Wooden frame: black, 11 x 14 inches (27.9 x 35.6 cm)

## INSTRUCTIONS

1. Copy or print out the Dancer pattern (page 114) onto black cardstock; cut out the shape with the craft knife.

2. Copy or print out the Black Frame pattern (page 114) onto black cardstock; cut out the shape with the craft knife.

3. Copy or print out the Parchment Backing pattern (page 114) onto parchment cardstock; cut out the shape with the craft knife.

4. Apply glue onto the black frame shape and adhere it to the parchment backing shape. Press firmly to ensure a strong bond.

5. Apply glue to the dancer shape, very carefully and in small amounts, and then adhere the dancer to the middle of the parchment backing shape.

6. Apply glue to the back of the parchment backing shape and adhere the shape to the center of the black mounting board. Press firmly to ensure a strong bond.

7. Place the finished piece in the frame.

# NEVER-TOO-LATE
# BOOK SCULPTURE

Jennifer Khoshbin

I HAVE BEEN WORKING with books as a sculptural material for some time. Paper is often a delicate form associated with a thin surface, but through book sculptures I am finding ways to present the conceptual depth of books. In addition to cuttings, I often add fine-line drawings or photo images to my sculptures to re-write the story. Because text is now most often viewed on a computer screen, I explore the future of the book itself, and try to imagine what it might be like for books to undergo a kind of adaptation for survival.

## TOOLS & MATERIALS

- Cardboard
- Circular paper cutting tool
- Craft glue
- Craft knife and extra blades
- Embellishments: collage, drawings, stamps, etc.
- Foamcore
- Hot glue gun
- Mat board
- Metal-edged ruler
- Old book
- Pencil
- Shadow box

## INSTRUCTIONS

*Note:* Choose the shadow box you will use first. Doing so will allow you to size your sculpture to fit inside it.

1. Remove the front and back covers (including the spine) of the book, leaving the binding glue intact to keep the pages bound together. Using the inside dimensions of the shadow box, measure, mark, and cut the bound pages so the book fits inside the frame. Cut the bound book pages to the correct dimensions with the metal-edged ruler and craft knife. *Note:* This will take some time depending on the thickness of the book. Do not worry if the book is smaller than the frame; the gap can be filled in later with foamcore.

2. Using the circular paper cutting tool, cut out the center of the book. *Note:* To cut out the circles, place a piece of cardboard under the first page of the book and cut away the circle with your cutting tool. Next, reduce the circle size of your cutting tool just a touch. Remove the cardboard and place it under the second page of the book; cut and remove the next circle. Continue cutting smaller and smaller circles until the book has been carved to its smallest circle.

3. Choose a meaningful word from the book's pages, cut it out, and glue it faceup on the first uncut page at the bottom of the removed circles. *Note:* Be sure to center the word so it can be read through the smallest cut circle.

4. Measure the inside of your shadow box and, with your craft knife, cut the mat board to those dimensions. Cut a circle in the center of the mat board to fit over your cut book pages. The easiest way to line this up is to tear the top sheet off of your book pages and use it as your stencil. Center this on your mat board, and trace the circle onto it. Using the circular cutting tool, cut and remove this circle from the mat board.

5. Decorate the mat board with drawings, collage materials, stamps, or a handwritten message.

6. Using the hot glue gun, secure the book pages in the frame. *Note:* The shadow box needs to be completely filled in to keep the project from shifting, so cut pieces of foamcore to fill in any gaps around the book pages and adhere with hot glue.

7. Adhere the mat board in place with craft glue.

Philip Simmons Gate on Orange Street
Charleston, SC
hand cut paper
Barbara Buckingham 2008

# ORANGE STREET & BROAD STREET GATES

Barbara Buckingham

**M**Y DESIGNS ARE DRIVEN by my love of the works of master metalsmiths, both past and present. The intent is to display my paper cuttings as ironwork and create awareness in the general public of both fine metalwork and the craft of paper cutting. Mr. Philip Simmons is my favorite living metalsmith and he is a national treasure. He has forged most of the ironwork in Charleston, South Carolina, within the past 70-plus years. Both of these framed gates are based on drawings I did of two of Simmons' gates in Charleston.

## TOOLS & MATERIALS

- Backing paper
- Clear acrylic or glass: 8 x 11 inches (20.3 x 27.9 cm) for the Orange Street Gate; 9 x 13 inches (22.9 x 33.0 cm) for the Broad Street Gate
- Computer and printer or copier
- Craft knife with #11 blade
- Foamcore: 12 x 15 inches (30.5 x 38.1 cm) for the Orange Street Gate; 13 x 17 inches (33.0 x 43.2 cm) for the Broad Street Gate (3 each)
- Frames and glass: 12 x 15 inches (30.5 x 38.1 cm) for the Orange Street Gate; 13 x 17 inches (33.0 x 43.2 cm) for the Broad Street Gate

- Framing points (for holding the work in the frame)
- Gem stones or beads (optional)
- Mat board: cream, 8 x 11 inches (20.3 x 27.9 cm) for the Orange Street Gate; black, 9 x 13 inches (22.9 x 33.0 cm) for the Broad Street Gate (3 each)
- Screw eyes
- Self-healing cutting mat
- Silhouette paper: two-sided black, 8 x 10 inches (20.3 x 25.4 cm) (2)
- Spray adhesive
- Tape
- Wire

# INSTRUCTIONS

*Note:* The method used is the same for both gates. Complete one gate at a time.

1. Print out or copy the Orange Street and Broad Street patterns (page 115) onto the white side of the silhouette paper. Place a piece of silhouette paper on the self-healing cutting mat, black side down.

2. Using the craft knife, cut out the shapes, working from the interior of the design. This will allow for any overcuts. After the piece is cut, prepare the mat board that it will be attached to by making sure it is free of dust or dirt.

3. Lay the gate cutting facedown on a piece of foamcore, masking areas that you do not want to glue with other small pieces of foamcore.

4. Spray the back of the gate with adhesive, and then carefully remove any masking.

5. To ready the gate for positioning on the mat board, pick up the lower right corner with your left index finger and thumb, lift it off the surface of the foamcore, and then grab the diagonal corner with your right index finger and thumb. Carefully position the lower left corner on the mat board, and then lower carefully toward the upper right corner. *Note:* I find this

step to be most critical because, once in position, there is no undoing it.

6. Once the gate is in position, carefully add gems or beads as desired. I used a bead for the gate handle. *Note:* For a more dimensional effect, gently lift some of the curled parts of the paper.

7. Cut out the center of two of the remaining pieces of foamcore, slightly larger than the glass. Leave one whole; this will be the back of the project.

8. Place the glass with the mounted paper cut on one of the cut pieces of foamcore, carefully making any further adjustments in centering, and tape it to the foamcore. Place this taped piece on top of the mat. Place the second piece of foamcore with the cutout center on top of that. Place the double mats on top of that, then the glass, and then finally the frame.

9. Secure the layers in the frame using the framing points, and then attach the backing paper, screw eyes, and wire. *Note:* If the instructions beyond step 7 seem too involved, you can just frame it at that point, or take it to a professional framer.

---

## CUTTING-EDGE ADVICE

The frames used in this project need to have a deep rabbet (the space from front of the inside of the frame to the back) to accommodate the glass, mats, and foamcore.

# THE TWINS

Cynthia Ferguson

THERE IS A PLAYFUL innocence to this piece. It reminds me of my first visit to my grandparents' home in Germany where I was intrigued by a framed paper cut. I used letter-weight paper to create The Twins and found it to be the perfect choice. Feel free to choose your own paper color. To finish the piece, consider mounting it on a contrasting color and then framing it.

## TOOLS & MATERIALS

- Computer and printer or copier
- Copy paper
- Craft knife or scissors
- Craft tape
- Letter-weight paper: 8½ x 11 inches (21.6 x 27.9 cm)
- Self-healing cutting mat

## INSTRUCTIONS

*Note:* This piece is a folded paper cut. The dotted line represents the fold of the paper. When unfolded, the mirror image of the pattern will be seen.

1. There are two ways to work with the pattern. You can copy or print out The Twins pattern (page 115) directly onto the letter-weight paper that is to be cut, and then fold the paper along the dotted line. Or, if you prefer, you can copy or print out the pattern onto copy paper, then trim around the edges of the pattern, leaving about a ½ inch (1.3 cm) of paper beyond the edges. Fold the letter-weight paper in half widthwise, then tape the pattern to the paper, making sure that the dotted line on the pattern meets the fold of the paper.

2. Cut out dark portions of the pattern first. *Note:* Do not cut through the dotted line; however, it is okay to remove the dark parts completely from the folded area.

3. Cut the outside edges of the pattern. Unfold the finished paper cut and enjoy.

# DOLLY

### La Donna Welter

CREATING A MAGICAL world from everyday materials has always fascinated me. The use of paper is no exception. Dolly is part of a paper cut series that features a magical world of little people living among flowers. It can be displayed in a deep-set frame or a shadow box.

## TOOLS & MATERIALS

- Acid-free glue stick, quick-dry adhesive
- Acid-free watercolor paper: #140, for base
- Computer and printer or copier
- Copy paper
- Craft knife with #11 blade
- Graphite transfer paper
- Pencil
- Self-healing cutting mat
- Small scissors
- Stylus: medium and large
- Toothpicks
- Tweezers

## INSTRUCTIONS

1. Copy or print out the Dolly patterns (page 116) onto copy paper and cut out the shapes, leaving about a ½-inch (1.3 cm) border outside the lines.

2. Using the pencil and graphite transfer paper, trace the patterns on the acid-free watercolor paper. Using scissors, cut out the flower petals and leaves. Using the craft knife, cut out smaller details including the stamens and stems.

3. Shape the petals using a stylus. (Use the medium stylus for smaller petals and a large stylus for larger petals.) Hold the stylus as if you are holding a pencil and begin moving the stylus in a circular "erasure" motion. The paper will start to take shape, curling and forming up around the stylus; continue until you achieve the desired shape.

4. After all petal pieces are formed, create each individual flower. To do this, use a small amount of quick-dry adhesive and a toothpick to glue each petal together at the base and then overlap them to form a flower. Once each flower is formed, add the stamens using a small amount of quick-dry adhesive and a toothpick. Hold the stamens in place with tweezers for a few seconds to allow the adhesive to set.

5. Form the leaves using the same method as for the petals, but move the stylus back and forth. Bend the leaves using your index finger and thumb for a more natural form.

6. Place the stems, leaves, and flowers on the base and glue in position, referring to the project photograph for placement. Adhere the child's silhouette using the glue stick.

# THE BEETLE'S DEVOTION

## Cynthia Ferguson

LOVE THE KINDNESS and innocence shown in this scene. Though I used neutral-colored paper, feel free to use colored cardstock when creating your project. The patterns can be reduced or enlarged to fit the frame size of your choice.

## TOOLS & MATERIALS

- Bone folder
- Cardstock: desired colors, 5½-inch (14 cm) square (1 sheet); 8½ x 11 inches (21.6 x 27.9 cm) (3 sheets)
- Computer and printer or copier
- Glue stick
- Scissors
- Shadow box: 5½-inch (14 cm) square

## INSTRUCTIONS

*Note:* These instructions are for shadow boxes that open from the back. If yours opens from the front, reverse the order of assembly.

1. Print out or copy The Beetle's Devotion, Beetle Background, and Beetle Foreground patterns (page 117) directly onto cardstock.

2. Cut out dark shapes first. Using the bone folder, score the dotted lines. Cut around the perimeter of each pattern, and then fold the pieces on the score marks. First fold in side flaps, then fold up bottom flap.

3. Using the glue stick, adhere the Beetle Foreground shape inside the shadow box. *Note:* The bottom right corner of the artwork should align with the bottom right corner of the shadow box.

4. Using the glue stick, adhere The Beetle's Devotion shapes inside the shadow box behind the Beetle Foreground. *Note:* The top left corner of this artwork should line up with the top left corner of the shadow box.

5. Using the glue stick, adhere the Beetle Background inside the shadow box. *Note:* This should be the very back of the scene.

6. Using the glue stick, adhere the 5½-inch (14 cm) square sheet of paper to the inside of the back of the shadow box. Close the back of the shadow box.

# BUTTERFLY GRAVE

Jennifer Khoshbin

T HIS PROJECT IS EASY to create and lends an elegant touch to any room. I always purchase the shadow box frame first—it is easier to size the book sculpture to fit inside the frame than to find a frame that fits the completed book sculpture. Though patterns are provided, wing shapes can be found online or in any insect book.

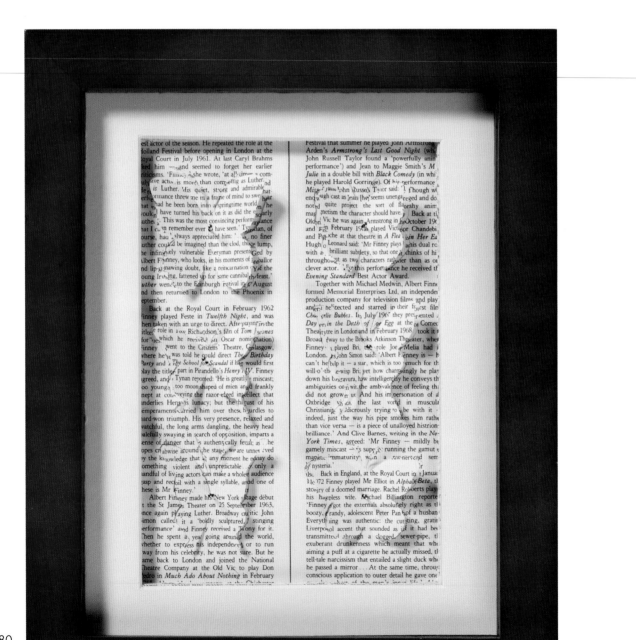

## TOOLS & MATERIALS

- Beveled-edge mat board cutter
- Cardboard or self-healing cutting mat
- Circular paper cutting tool
- Computer and printer or copier
- Copy paper
- Craft glue
- Craft knife
- Foamcore: white
- Hot glue gun
- Mat board
- Metal-edged ruler
- Old book
- Pencil
- Scissors
- Shadow box
- Straight pins

## INSTRUCTIONS

*Note:* These instructions are for shadow boxes that open from the front. If yours opens from the back, reverse the order of assembly—mat board window in first, followed by the cut book pages, etc.

1. Print out or copy the Butterfly pattern (page 116) six times onto copy paper. Cut out the shapes.

2. Remove the front and back covers from the book, including the spine. Leave the binding glue intact in order to keep the pages bound together. Using the inside dimensions of the shadow box, measure, mark, and cut the bound pages of the book so it fits inside the shadow box. *Note:* Do not worry if the book is smaller than the frame; any gaps can be filled in later with foamcore.

3. Using the craft knife and metal-edged ruler, cut the bound book pages to fit inside the shadow box. Evenly space the Butterfly patterns on the top page of the book. Using the pencil, trace around the shapes then remove the patterns.

4. Place a piece of cardboard or small self-healing cutting mat under the first page of the book and cut around the wings and antennas. *Note:* Be sure to keep a small uncut area between each wing so the butterflies remain connected to the page.

5. Fold the wings toward one another so they lift off the page. Push a pin into the center of each pair of wings to simulate a butterfly collection.

6. Using the mat board cutter, cut the mat board the same dimensions as the inside of the shadow box. Using the metal ruler and the top page of the book, determine how large the mat board "window" needs to be. Using the mat board cutter, cut out the center of the mat board to the desired size.

7. Using the hot glue gun, adhere the back and sides of the book to the shadow box. Using the craft knife, cut pieces of foamcore to fill in any gaps then glue the pieces in place with the hot glue gun. Using craft glue, adhere the mat board window to the top of the book. Close the shadow box.

*Chapter 5*

# FOR GIVE AND TAKE

THE ART OF SAYING THANK YOU is well-suited to paper cutting. There is no better way to let someone know you care than to give him or her a handmade token of appreciation. The time spent and care taken to create your gift will bring smiles to all those lucky enough to receive such an item.

Cards are perhaps the most obvious thank you. In today's world of email, blogs, and social networking via the Internet, receiving a hand-crafted card is a special occasion in itself. Instead of putting small gifts like candy or jewelry in a plain box, present them in a unique treat cone. Embellish the cone with ribbon and it can be tied to a chair or hung on a doorknob. Transform boxes and bags with elegant embellishments.

The projects in this chapter were created to express gratitude in a variety of ways. Karin Marlett Choi made a gorgeous pop-up card. Cynthia Ferguson created a treat cone perfect for any occasion. Nicole Lombardo's embellishments transform plain packages into original works of art.

On the following pages are projects that will inspire you and allow you to give special thanks to the people in your life.

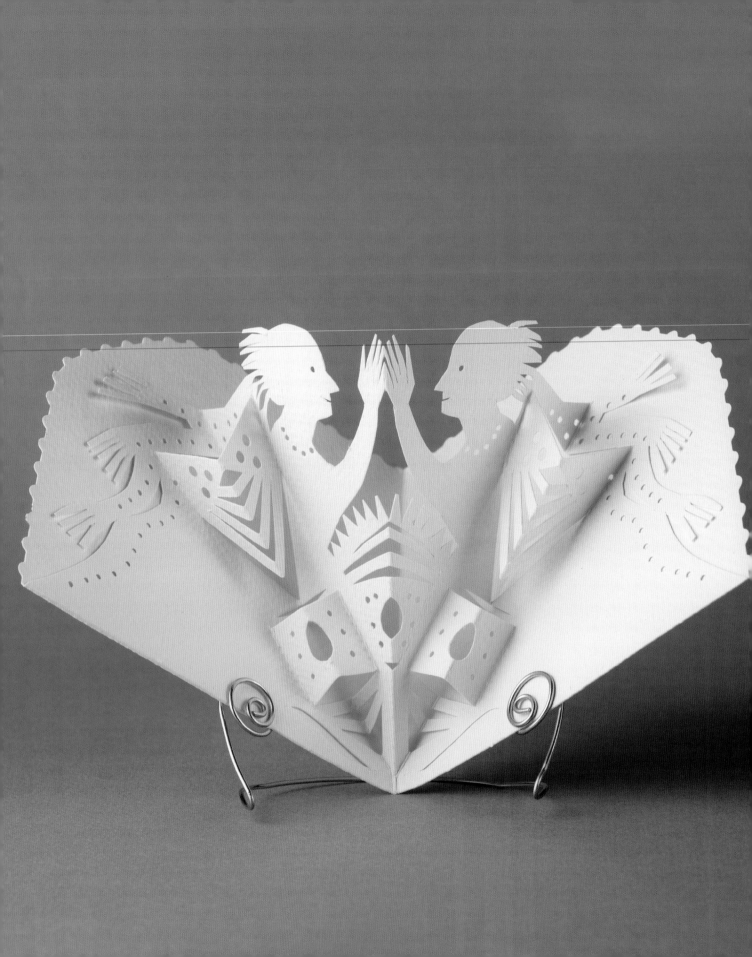

# K I R I G A M I   C A R D

Cynthia Emerlye

THIS KIRIGAMI CARD is fun to create and receive. Though I have created a white card, feel free to make yours with colored paper. The outside of the card can be decorated with rubber stamps, as shown above, or embellished with paint, rhinestones, or other materials.

✂ - - - - - - - - - - - - - - - - - - - - - - - - - - - - - - - - - - - - - - - -

## TOOLS & MATERIALS

- Acid-free permanent glue
- Bone folder
- Cardstock: 8½-inch (21.6 cm) square
- Circular paper punch or awl: 1/16 inch (1.5 mm)
- Computer and printer or copier
- Copy paper
- Craft knife with #11 blade
- Heavy books

- Inkpad
- Letter-weight paper: 8-inch (20.3 cm) square
- Pencil
- Rubber stamps
- Scissors
- Scrap paper
- Soft eraser
- Tracing paper

## INSTRUCTIONS

*Note:* Fig. 1 (page 87) illustrates the paper square as it is referred to in the following instructions.

1. Copy or print out the Kirigami Card pattern (page 116) onto copy paper.

2. Fold the square of paper in half, bottom edge B to top edge A, and crease well with the bone folder (Fig. 2, page 87).

3. Open the piece of paper, then fold it in half again, side edge C to side edge D, and crease well with the bone folder. Your paper will now be a tall rectangle that looks like two squares on top of each other (Figs. 3a and 3b, page 87).

4. Fold the bottom square diagonally, the bottom left corner B to the middle right C (Fig. 4). The resulting fold creates a line marked by the letters X and E. Open the fold. Notice that the top portion looks like a square and the bottom portion looks like two triangles. The top portion makes up the front and back of the card.

5. To make the top edge of the card, lightly trace an arc from point A to point C and cut along the arc with scissors (Fig. 5). *Note:* You may wish to use a circle pattern, protractor, or cup to help you draw an even arc.

6. Open the paper so you can see the entire square; the top edge should be curved. Fold the top edge down to the bottom edge B. Cut off any excess paper along the bottom edge B so that the top and bottom edges are aligned (Figs. 6a and 6b).

7. Holding the paper horizontally like an open book, slowly and carefully close the card, folding side C to side D, while making sure that points E and F fold back and that the center fold B-X pops out toward the front (Fig. 7). This is basically how your card will open when you are finished. *Note:* Do not use the bone folder or press down hard when arranging these folds as doing so will leave a crease down the face of the card.

8. Open the card again so that the uncreased square is on the bottom and the creased part is on the top. Point X should be on the middle left (Fig. 8). *Note:* This is the position in which you will hold the paper while cutting out the design.

9. Very lightly trace the pattern design onto the upper half of the shape and cut out the outer edges of the design using scissors and the craft knife on the interior portions (Fig. 9). *Note:* Be careful to not cut into the bottom half of the shape.

10. When you are finished cutting out the design, fold over the top triangle. Fold tabs G and H, pressing them back and forth to form folds (Fig. 10). This will be the pop-up part of the card.

## To complete front of card

1. Unfold the card part way so you have a long rectangle. Place clean scrap paper under and inside the card, as well as over the bottom portion of the front of the rectangle (Fig. 11).

2. Stamp the top edge of the card with a design; let the ink dry completely before proceeding.

3. Once the ink is dry, refold the paper, as shown in Fig. 2. The cut-out portions should be facing you. Apply glue to the left and right bottom inside portions of the card, leaving the center portions unglued (Fig. 12).

## To finish card

1. Immediately place the card between several heavy books until the glue is completely dry. (It will take several hours to dry.)

2. When the glue is dry, gently fold the card closed, making sure to pop out the center designs and the tabs to create a dimensional effect. Do not press down hard on the fold, as doing so will leave a crease down the front of the card.

### CUTTING-EDGE ADVICE

It is important to test the folding quality of the paper you choose. The paper must be sturdy enough for the paper cut design, yet pliable enough to not crack when folding. Fold samples of your desired papers to see how workable they are prior to using them in any project.

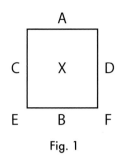

Fig. 1

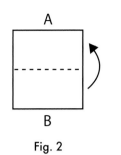

Fig. 2

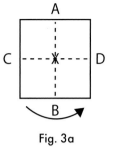

Fig. 3a

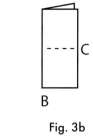

Fig. 3b

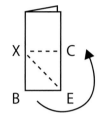

Fig. 4

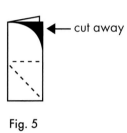

cut away

Fig. 5

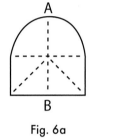

Fig. 6a

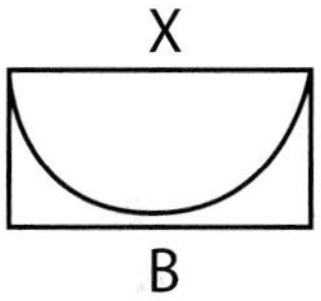

Fig. 6b

Fig. 7

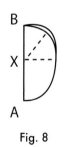

Fig. 8

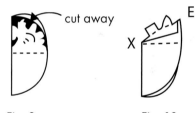

cut away

Fig. 9

Fig. 10

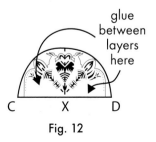

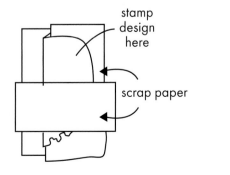

stamp design here

scrap paper

Fig. 11

glue between layers here

Fig. 12

# FLOWERS & BUTTERFLY CARD

Tina Tarnoff

THIS CARD CAN BE USED for any occasion. It is quite striking in its simplicity and two-tone color scheme. You will need a bit of patience to complete this project, but the final result is well worth the effort. When working on a detailed project such as this one, I often practice cutting the design on scrap paper.

## TOOLS & MATERIALS

- Cardstock: black, cream, 4¼ x 5½ inches (10.8 x 14 cm) (1 each); cream, 5½ x 8½ inches (14 x 21.6 cm)
- Computer and printer or copier
- Copy paper
- Craft knife
- Glue pen
- Graphite transfer paper
- Paper trimmer with curved blades
- Pencil
- Self-healing cutting mat
- Tweezers

## INSTRUCTIONS

1. Copy or print out the Flowers and Butterfly pattern (page 117) onto copy paper. Using the graphite transfer paper, trace the pattern onto the 4¼ x 5½-inch (10.8 x 14 cm) piece of cream cardstock; cut out the shape with the craft knife.

2. Using the paper trimmer, cut ⅜ inch (0.9 cm) from each side of the 4¼ x 5½-inch (10.8 x 14 cm) black cardstock.

3. Fold the 5½ x 8½-inch (14 x 21.6 cm) piece of cream cardstock in half lengthwise, creating the card.

4. Apply glue to the back of the 4¼ x 5½-inch (10.8 x 14 cm) piece of black cardstock and adhere it to the center of the front of the card.

5. Apply glue to the back of the flowers and butterfly shape. *Note:* Use the adhesive sparingly so the glue does not ooze out from the sides of the shape.

6. Using the tweezers, carefully lift the flowers and butterfly shape off the work surface and adhere them to the front of the card, using the project photograph for reference.

# BIRD OF PARADISE IKEBANA POP-UP CARD

Karin Marlett Choi

THIS LAYERED CARD ILLUSTRATES how negative space can be essential to a paper cut design. I like creating movement and dimension with my designs, as evidenced in the flower vase portion of the card. The patterns are precisely spaced, so it is important to follow the instructions carefully.

## TOOLS & MATERIALS

- Bone folder
- Cardstock: purple, 4¼ x 11 inches (10.8 x 27.9 cm); cream, 4 x 10½ inches (10.2 x 26.7 cm)
- Computer and printer or copier
- Copy paper

- Craft knife with #11 blade
- Glue stick
- Graphite transfer paper
- Pencil
- Scrap paper
- Self-healing cutting mat

## INSTRUCTIONS

1. Print out or copy the Cover and Inside patterns (page 118) onto copy paper.

2. Fold the purple cardstock in half widthwise so you have a 4¼ x 5½-inch (10.8 x 14 cm) card.

3. Fold the cream cardstock in half widthwise so you have a 4 x 5¼-inch (10.2 x 13.3 cm) card.

4. Open the purple card so that it lays flat. Using the graphite transfer paper, trace the Cover pattern onto the bottom left corner of the inside of the card. Using the craft knife, cut out the shape.

5. Open the cream card so it lays flat. Using transfer paper, trace the Inside pattern onto the top half of the inside of the cream card. Using the craft knife, cut out the flower arrangement. Do not cut out the vase shape at this time.

6. Fold the cream card in half and use the craft knife to cut the lines of the vase, cutting through both layers of the card. With the card still folded, crease each strip back, one by one, so they will splay out along the contour of the vase. Carefully open the card. Using your fingers, gently press the vertical strips of the vase toward the inside of the card; close the card. Using the bone folder, burnish the contour of the vase from the back to reinforce the creases.

7. Spread a strip of glue on the back of the top and bottom edges of the cream card. Center and glue the cream card inside the purple card, making sure that the paper cut flower on the purple card is on the right side of the front of the card. Lay a piece of scrap paper on top of the card and burnish the surface of the card using the bone folder.

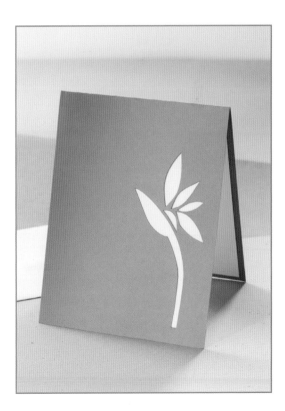

# INITIAL GIFT TAG

Cynthia Ferguson

THIS PRETTY GIFT TAG turns ordinary gift wrap into something special. To give the tag a dimensional look, I affixed each of the pieces with foam dots. Using cardstock in a variety of colors adds a nice contrast.

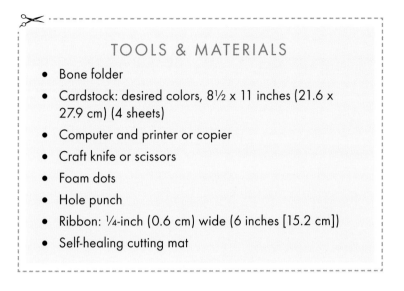

## TOOLS & MATERIALS

- Bone folder
- Cardstock: desired colors, 8½ x 11 inches (21.6 x 27.9 cm) (4 sheets)
- Computer and printer or copier
- Craft knife or scissors
- Foam dots
- Hole punch
- Ribbon: ¼-inch (0.6 cm) wide (6 inches [15.2 cm])
- Self-healing cutting mat

## INSTRUCTIONS

1. Print out or copy the Gift Tag, Alphabet, Background, and Tag Bird patterns (page 119). Print each pattern onto a separate piece of cardstock.

2. Using the bone folder, score and fold the Gift Tag and Tag Bird patterns along the dotted lines.

3. Using the craft knife or scissors, cut out the Gift Tag, Background, and Tag Bird shapes. Choose desired letter and cut out. Unfold the Tag Bird shape. Using the hole punch, make a hole at the top of the tag.

4. Center the background shape on the front of the gift tag and adhere with foam dots. Center desired letter on background shape and adhere with foam dots.

5. To attach the bird, fold the gift tag and tag bird shapes in half (the half mark on the bird is the center of the heart). Fold the bird back behind itself on each side at fold line between the beak and the heart. Slide the folded bird inside the card with the folded heart portion facing the crease of the card. Do not position the bird fold line flush with the card fold line; instead, ease it out about ¼ inch (0.6 cm) away from the crease of the card. In this position, affix the tail to each side of the card.

6. Place the ribbon through the holes and tie the tag to the gift.

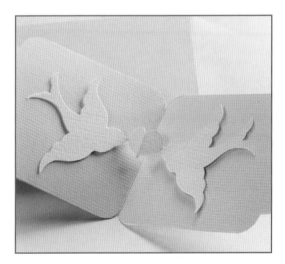

# FRAMES &
# EMBELLISHMENTS

Nicole Lombardo

USE THESE PRETTY FRAMES and embellishments around pictures, in scrapbooks, and on cards, gift bags, and gift boxes. They also look lovely when placed on a picture mat. Feel free to embellish the paper cuts with gems, rhinestones, stamps, and other materials.

## TOOLS & MATERIALS

- Cardstock: desired colors, 8½ x 11 inches (21.6 x 27.9 cm)
- Computer and printer or copier
- Craft knife or scissors
- Self-healing cutting mat

## INSTRUCTIONS

1. Copy or print out the Flower Frame, Scroll Frame, Scroll A, Scroll B, and Bluebird patterns (page 120) onto the cardstock.

2. Using the craft knife or scissors, carefully cut out the shapes. They are now ready for use.

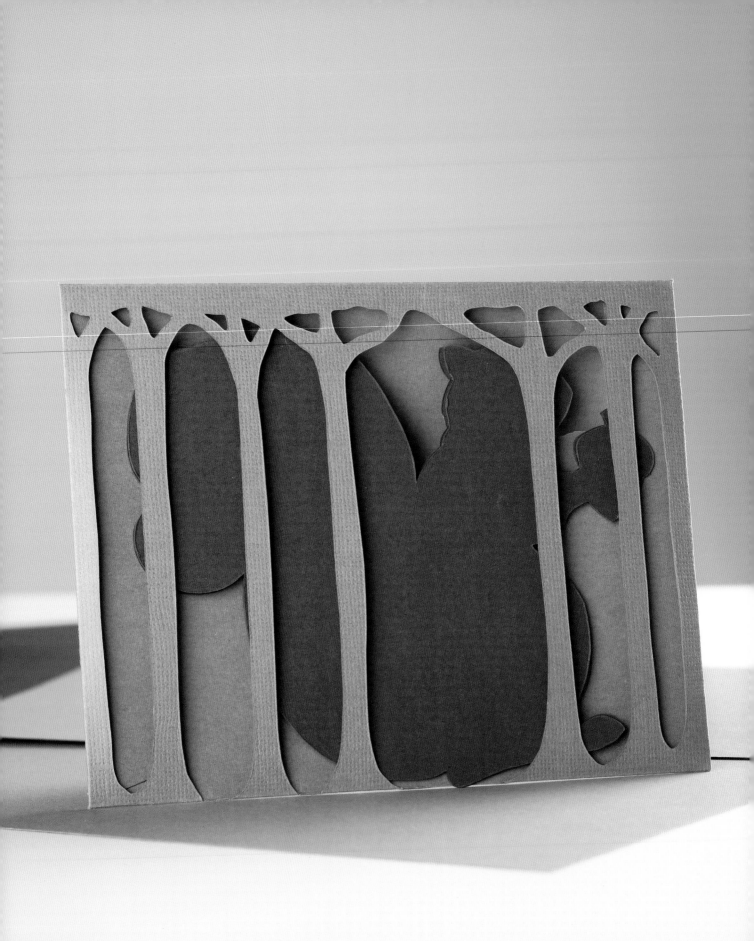

# SQUIRREL IN THE WOODS CARD & ENVELOPE

Cynthia Ferguson

THE WHIMSICAL FOREST theme of this card-and-envelope set is sure to bring a smile to its recipient. Use a gel pen or fine-point paint pen to write on the squirrel. To mail the card and envelope, I insert them in a plain, uncut envelope for addressing and transit.

## TOOLS & MATERIALS

- Bone folder
- Cardstock: brown, green, 8½ x 11 inches (21.6 x 27.9 cm) (1 each)
- Computer and printer or copier
- Craft knife or scissors
- Glue stick
- Self-healing cutting mat

## INSTRUCTIONS

*To make card*

1. Copy or print out the Squirrel pattern (page 121) onto the brown cardstock. Using the bone folder, score the cardstock along the dotted line.

2. Cut out the squirrel shape; cut out the gray shapes first, then cut the edges of the pattern. *Note:* Do not cut along the dotted line; this is where the card will fold.

3. Fold the card along the dotted line, reinforcing the fold with the bone folder.

*To make envelope*

1. Copy or print out the Envelope pattern (page 121) onto the green cardstock. Cut out the interior shapes.

2. Using the bone folder, score along the dotted lines.

3. Cut around the perimeter of the pattern.

4. Fold the cardstock on the score lines. Fold in the side flaps, then fold up the bottom flap.

5. Adhere the bottom flap to the side flaps with glue; allow the glue to dry.

6. Insert the card into the envelope and seal with glue.

# FEATHERED FRIENDS
# TREAT CONE

Cynthia Ferguson

THIS SIMPLE CONE is all dressed up and ready to fill. Add some candy and hang it on the back of a dining chair as a gift for your guest, or use it to hold bits of ribbon in a craft room. You can even fill it with a small bouquet of vintage silk flowers and hang it on a doorknob for display. I have created this basic cone for many different occasions—I just alter the cutout design. To use your own cutout design, simply trace it onto the cone pattern.

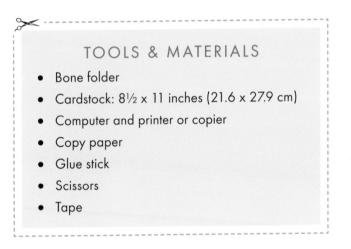

## TOOLS & MATERIALS

- Bone folder
- Cardstock: 8½ x 11 inches (21.6 x 27.9 cm)
- Computer and printer or copier
- Copy paper
- Glue stick
- Scissors
- Tape

## INSTRUCTIONS

*Note:* Dotted lines represent the folds of the paper; do not cut these.

1. There are two ways to work with the pattern. You can copy or print out the Treat Cone pattern (page 117) directly onto the cardstock or you can copy or print out the pattern onto copy paper, then trim around the edges of the pattern, leaving about a ½-inch (1.3 cm) border of paper beyond the edges. Tape the pattern to the cardstock.

2. Cut out gray portions of the pattern first, and then cut the outside lines.

3. Score the dotted lines with a bone folder and fold the cardstock, referring to the project photograph if needed.

4. Slip the flap behind the cone's side edge and adhere together using the glue stick.

# THE FROG PRINCE

Cynthia Ferguson

I BASED THIS PROJECT on one of my favorite stories. The scene portrayed in the box shows the act of giving and is perfect for a thank-you gift. To add interest to the front of the box, consider cutting out an extra Frog Prince Flowers pattern and adhering it to the box with glue dots.

## TOOLS & MATERIALS

- Bone folder
- Cardstock: desired colors, 6-inch (15.2 cm) square (1 sheet); 8½ x 11 inches (21.6 x 27.9 cm) (3 sheets)
- Computer and printer or copier
- Glue stick
- Papier-mâché box: 6-inch (15.2 cm) square with cutout window
- Scissors

## INSTRUCTIONS

1. Print out or copy the Frog Prince, Frog Prince Flowers, and Frog Prince Trees patterns (pages 122–123) directly onto cardstock.

2. Cut out the dark shapes on each of the patterns. Using the bone folder, score along the dotted lines. Cut around the perimeter of each pattern. Fold each shape on the score marks and then fold in the flaps.

3. Using the glue stick, adhere the 6-inch (15.2 cm) square sheet of paper to the inside bottom of the box.

4. Using the glue stick, adhere the flap of the Frog Prince Flowers shape on the bottom of the frame, referring to the project photograph.

5. Using the glue stick, adhere the flap of the Frog Prince shape to the bottom of the box, referring to the project photograph. *Note:* The back of the tab should be flush with the back of the frame.

6. Using the glue stick, adhere the Frog Prince Trees bottom tabs and the top tabs to the inside of the box, referring to the project photograph. *Note:* The back of the tabs should be flush with the back of the frame.

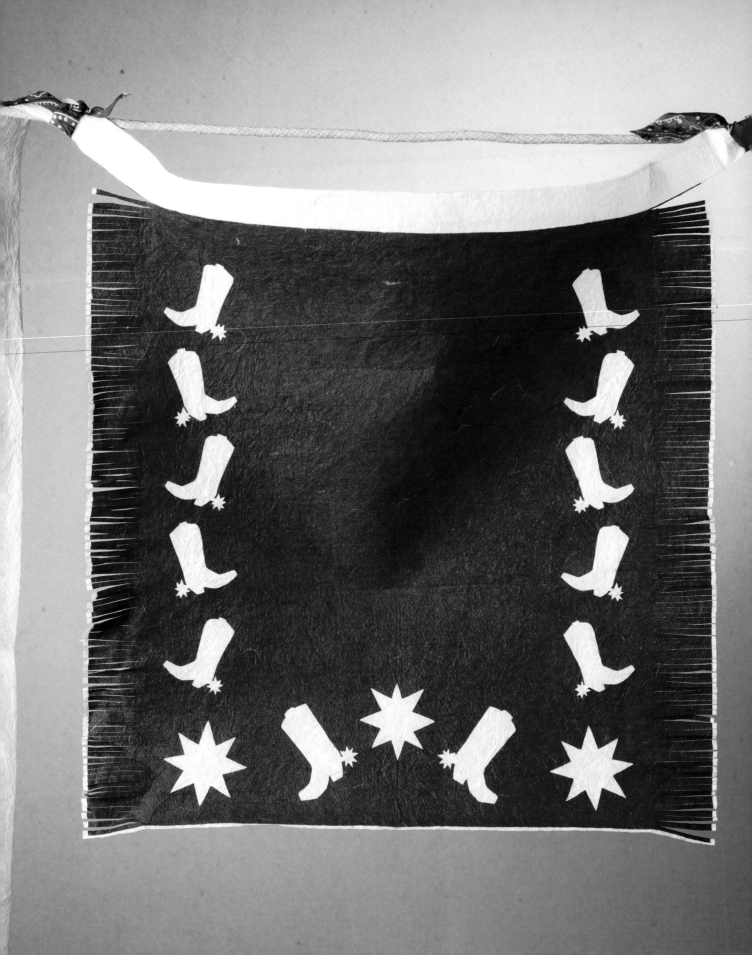

# COWGIRL APRON

## Holly Christian

T HE THAI SOFT UNRYU papers I used to create this project are quite strong and have the look and feel of fabric. The apron would be a wonderful hostess gift. Feel free to use different colors of the Thai paper to create your apron.

## TOOLS & MATERIALS

- Copy paper: 11 x 17 inches (27.9 x 43.2 cm)
- Craft knife
- Glue stick
- Iron with dry setting
- Large paper clips (5–6)
- Metal-edged ruler
- Pencil
- Scissors
- Self-healing cutting mat
- Spray adhesive
- Thai soft Unryu paper: burgundy, white, 23 x 34 inches (58.4 x 86.4 cm) (1 each)
- Tissue paper: white

## INSTRUCTIONS

*Note:* The finished apron is about 16 inches (40.6 cm) square with 33-inch (83.8 cm) ties.

1. Iron the Thai soft Unryu paper to flatten it and remove any wrinkles. *Note:* Usually a dry iron will suffice, but if the paper is especially wrinkled, use the lowest steam setting to iron the paper.

2. Copy or print out the Cowgirl Apron pattern (page 124) onto the copy paper.

3. Cut one 17-inch (43.2 cm) square piece of burgundy Thai soft Unryu paper.

4. Cut one 17-inch (43.2 cm) square piece, two 3 x 34-inch (7.6 x 86.4 cm) pieces, and one 3 x 17-inch (7.6 x 43.2 cm) piece of white Thai soft Unryu paper. Set these pieces aside.

5. Fold the burgundy Thai soft Unryu paper in half and place the pattern on top, lining up the pattern fold with the paper fold. Secure the pattern to the paper with paper clips.

6. Using the craft knife, carefully cut out the boot and spur shapes.

7. Using the metal-edged ruler and craft knife, trim the edges of the burgundy Thai soft Unryu paper as shown on the pattern.

8. Unfold the burgundy Thai soft Unryu paper and clean up any cuts with the craft knife.

9. Place a piece of tissue paper on top and under the cut burgundy Thai soft Unryu paper and press flat with the iron using a dry setting.

**10.** Apply spray adhesive to one side of the 17-inch (43.2 cm) square piece of white Thai soft Unryu paper. Carefully place the cut burgundy Thai soft Unryu paper in the middle of the sticky side of the white Thai soft Unryu paper and smooth flat with your hands. *Note:* If everything gets stuck together, patiently pull the pieces apart. Thai soft Unryu paper is quite strong; even when disaster seems imminent, it will come apart.

**11.** Place a piece of tissue paper on top and under the burgundy-and-white piece, and then carefully iron the piece to flatten.

**12.** Trim the edges of the burgundy-and-white piece with the metal ruler and craft knife, leaving a ⅛-inch (0.3 cm) edge of white paper showing along the bottom and sides. Set this piece aside.

**13.** To create the tie, attach the three pieces of 3-inch (7.6 cm) wide white Thai soft Unryu paper together lengthwise using the glue stick. Overlap each strip by 1 inch (2.5 cm) or so when gluing.

**14.** Fold the tie in thirds lengthwise and glue one end of the flap down with the glue stick.

**15.** Find the middle of the tie strip and lay that section horizontally on the top backside of the burgundy-and-white piece, and secure with the glue stick.

**16.** Trim the ties on each side to about 33 inches (83.8 cm) long.

**17.** To cut the fringe on the sides of the apron, measure 1½ inches (3.8 cm) in from each side, and then cut ⅛-inch (0.3 cm) strips along the edges.

## FLAG
*Enlarge 150%*

## MANDALA
*Actual size*

## INVITATION
*Enlarge 150%*

### CENTERPIECE A
*Enlarge 300%*

### CENTERPIECE B
*Enlarge 300%*

# PLACE CARDS
*Enlarge 200%*

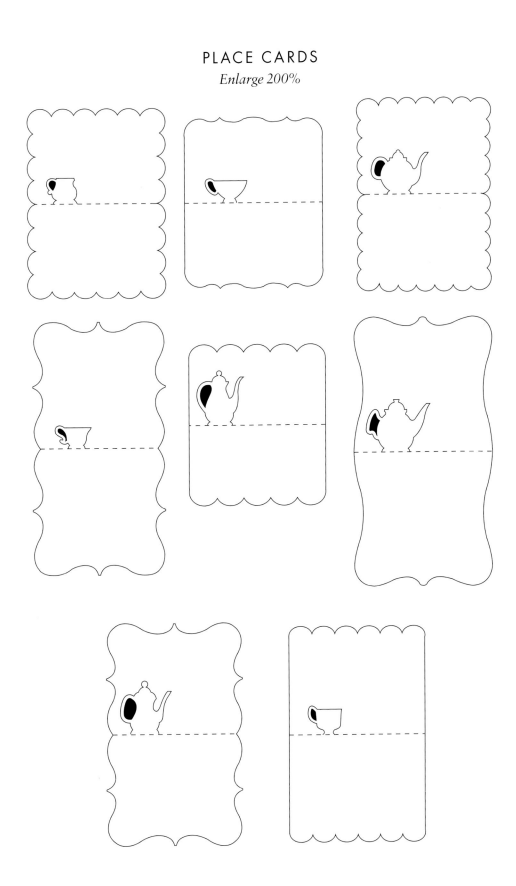

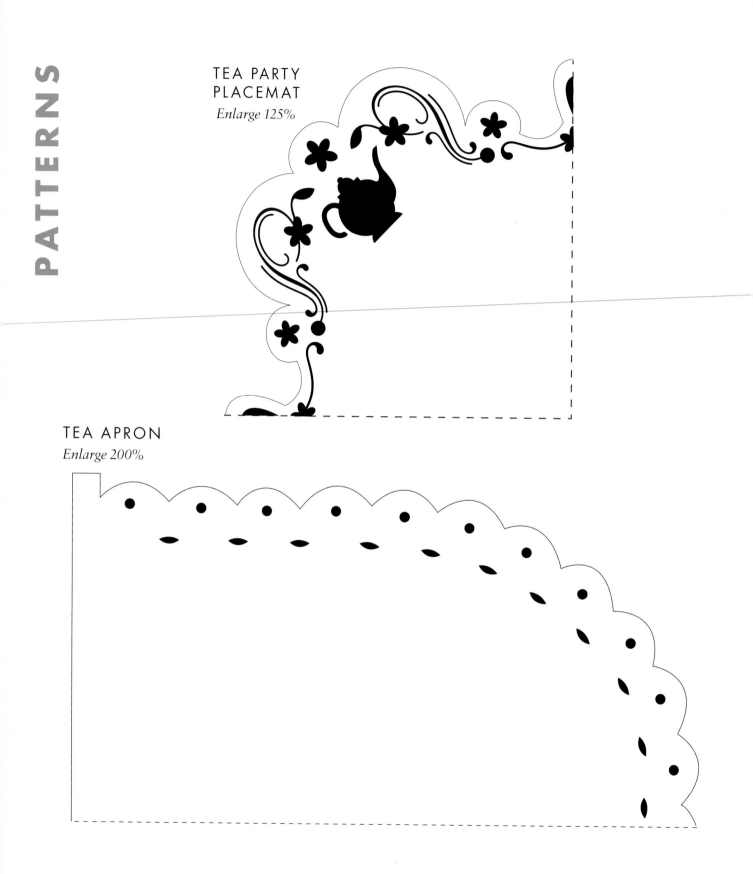

PATTERNS

TEA PARTY
PLACEMAT
*Enlarge 125%*

TEA APRON
*Enlarge 200%*

## TABLE RUNNER
*Enlarge 250%*

## BIRD
*Enlarge 250%*

## ACORN LUMINARY
*Enlarge 400%*

## FRAMES
*Enlarge 400%*

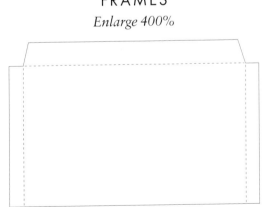

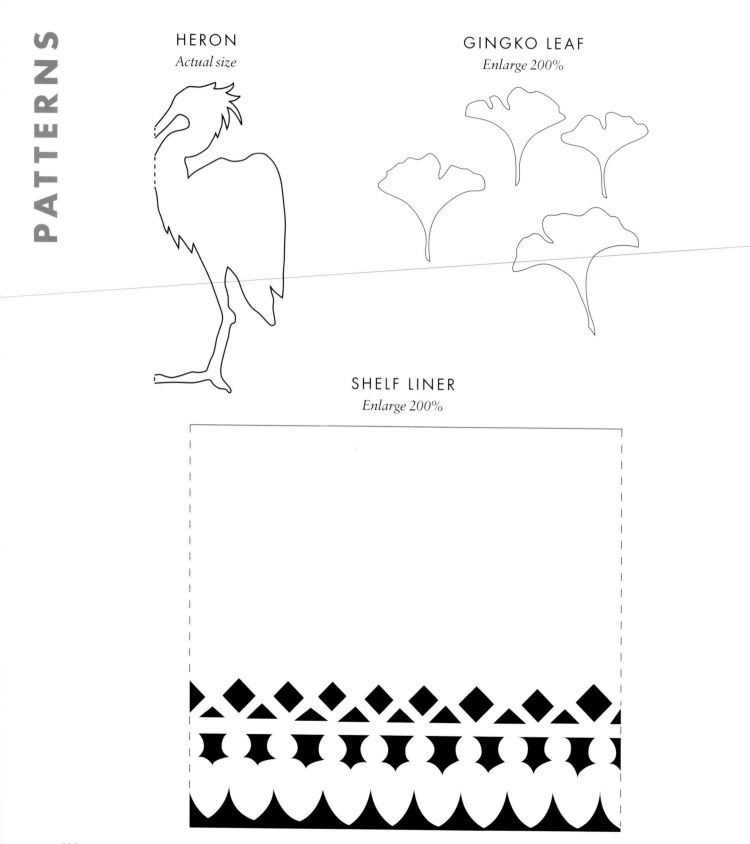

# PATTERNS

### HERON
*Actual size*

### GINGKO LEAF
*Enlarge 200%*

### SHELF LINER
*Enlarge 200%*

### FOREST A
*Enlarge 250%*

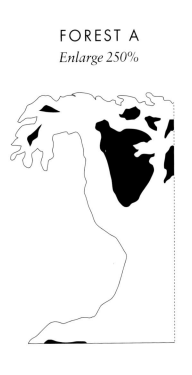

### FOREST B
*Enlarge 250%*

### FOREST C
*Enlarge 250%*

### FOREST D
*Enlarge 250%*

### FOREST E
*Enlarge 250%*

### FOREST F
*Enlarge 250%*

# VALANCE
*Enlarge 625%*

## LARGE FLOWER
*Enlarge 150%*

## FAIRIES
*Actual size*

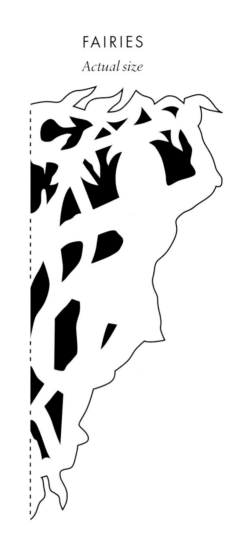

## BUD
*Actual size*

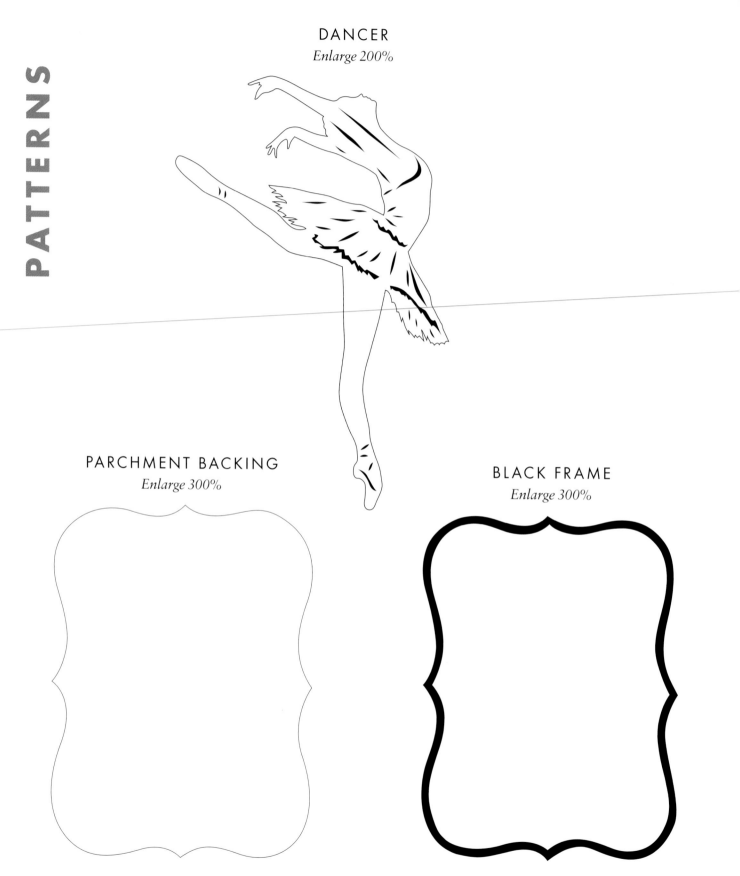

# PATTERNS

**DANCER**
*Enlarge 200%*

**PARCHMENT BACKING**
*Enlarge 300%*

**BLACK FRAME**
*Enlarge 300%*

## ORANGE STREET
*Enlarge 200%*

## THE TWINS
*Actual size*

## BROAD STREET
*Enlarge 200%*

115

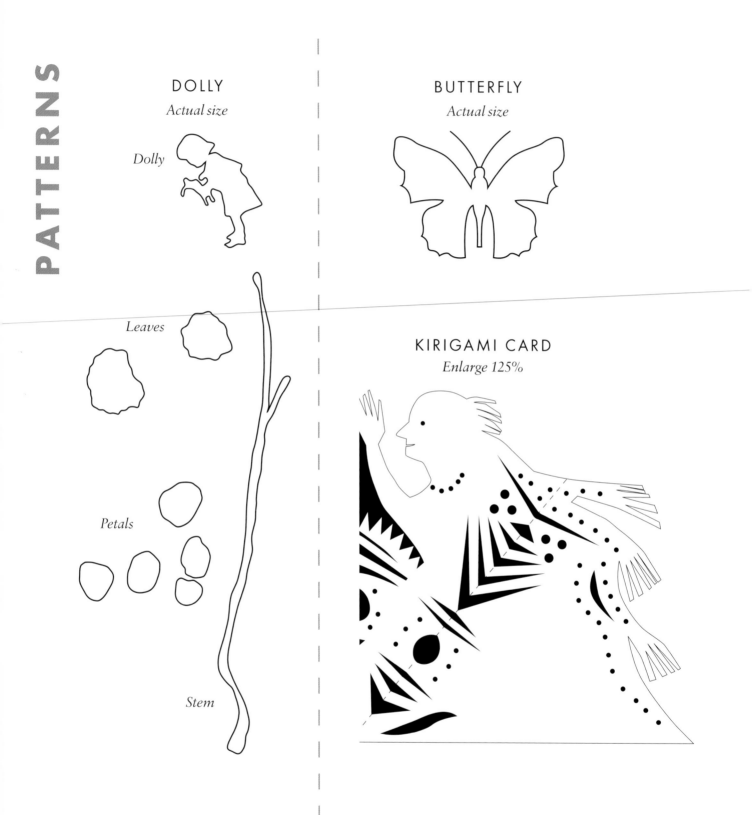

### DOLLY
*Actual size*

Dolly

### BUTTERFLY
*Actual size*

Leaves

Petals

Stem

### KIRIGAMI CARD
*Enlarge 125%*

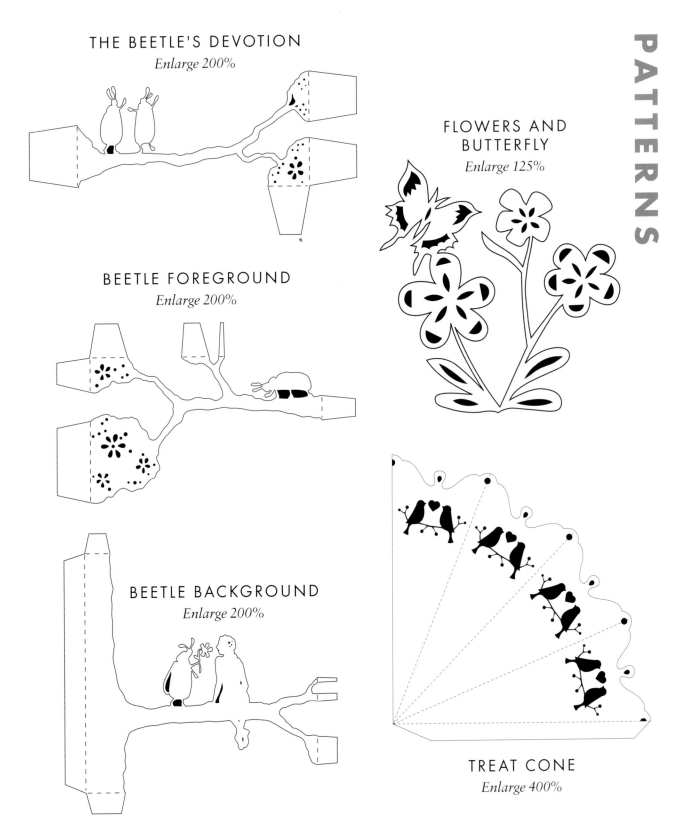

# THE BEETLE'S DEVOTION
*Enlarge 200%*

# BEETLE FOREGROUND
*Enlarge 200%*

# BEETLE BACKGROUND
*Enlarge 200%*

# FLOWERS AND BUTTERFLY
*Enlarge 125%*

# TREAT CONE
*Enlarge 400%*

COVER
*Enlarge 150%*

INSIDE
*Enlarge 150%*

## ALPHABET
*Enlarge 200%*

## GIFT TAG
*Enlarge 200%*

## BACKGROUND
*Enlarge 125%*

## TAG BIRD
*Actual size*

**PATTERNS**

**SCROLL FRAME**
*Enlarge 200%*

**FLOWER FRAME**
*Enlarge 200%*

**SCROLL A**
*Enlarge 150%*

**BLUEBIRD**
*Enlarge 125%*

**SCROLL B**
*Enlarge 150%*

## ENVELOPE
*Enlarge 200%*

## SQUIRREL
*Enlarge 200%*

# FROG PRINCE TREES
*Actual size*

## FROG PRINCE FLOWERS
*Enlarge 125%*

## FROG PRINCE
*Enlarge 125%*

# COWGIRL APRON

*Enlarge 200%*

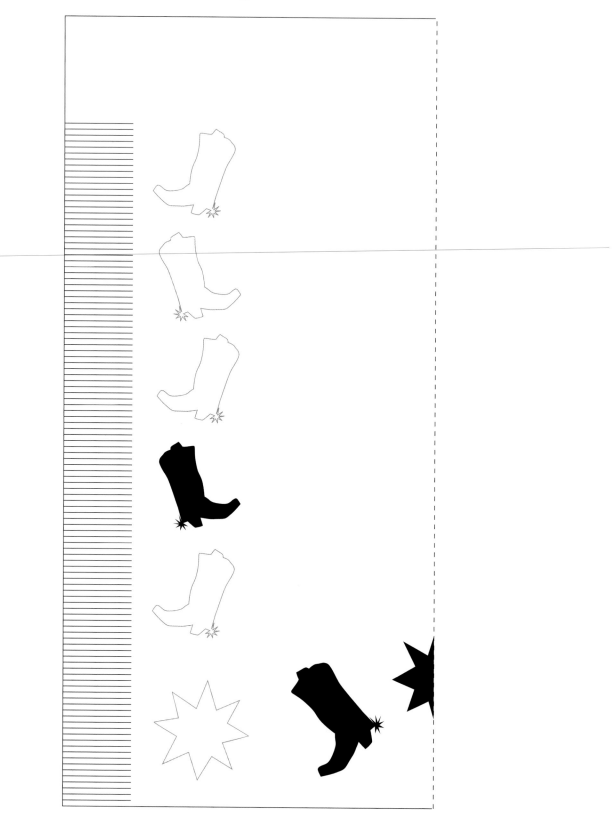

# Meet the Designers

## BARBARA BUCKINGHAM

Barbara Buckingham's paper cuts reflect her fascination and respect for the exquisite ironwork found in the south and southeastern United States. She strives for authenticity with her interpretations of noteworthy and historic gates.

Barbara began cutting paper in the German tradition, but found her passion after receiving a commission to execute an iron gate in paper. Barbara says she especially enjoys the strength of black and white and the power of negative space, and feels that her pieces preserve the craft of paper cutting and the beauty of ironwork.

Growing up in an artistic environment, Barbara was taught many skills by her mother and was encouraged to pursue her own creative path. Through the years she has worked in a variety of mediums including cross stitch, faux finishing, needlework, pencil sketching, and watercolor. See more of Barbara's work at papergates.com.

## KARIN MARLETT CHOI

Karin Marlett Choi manipulates paper from her studio in Rochester, New York. She loves the snowy months and attributes that to her love of cutting paper snowflakes. She holds degrees in graphic art and studio art and is often dabbling in new media. While growing up, her mother was always making things from paper and she exposed Karin to various forms of paper cutting including origami, scherenschnitte, and kirigami. Armed with a craft blade and cutting mat, Karin explores structuring paper through creating pop-ups and home décor. See more of Karin's work at karinmarlettchoi.com and intertwingle.etsy.com.

## HOLLY CHRISTIAN

Holly Christian has a background in art, drafting, rug weaving, dyeing, and beadwork. A few years ago she fell into her perfect job: coming up with craft projects and writing about them. Holly loves the challenge of creating something practical or beautiful with common, everyday materials used in new ways. Holly has been a craft editor for *HGTV Ideas* magazine, and has appeared on diynetwork.com. See more of Holly's work at hollychristian.com.

## CYNTHIA EMERLYE

Cynthia Emerlye was born in Rhode Island. Growing up in a creative, traveling family, she was introduced to crafting at a young age. Sewing, knitting, crocheting, painting, drawing, carving, building, cooking, and canning—all were taught to her by her grandparents and parents. She is married and the mother of six grown children. Cynthia now spends her days working in her home studio in Vermont. She dabbles in many different mediums including painting, illustration, and design, and has a self-proclaimed love affair with paper. She has been creating paper art for decades and is an expert kirigami craftsman. See more of Cynthia's work at emerlyearts.com, emerlyearts.blogspot.com, and emerlyeartskirigami.etsy.com.

## CYNTHIA FERGUSON

Cynthia Ferguson became interested in paper cutting while visiting her grandparents' home in Germany. In their sitting room they had a few paper cuts hanging on the wall. The pieces were so intricate and beautiful she knew that she would have to give it a try. She has been working in graphic design for more than 10 years and has been paper cutting for just the last few years. Her most elaborate project to date is a series of eight large paper cuts featuring historical events at the Tower of London. The series is currently on display in the Tower of London Children's Education Room in London. See more of Cynthia's work at cindyferguson.com, cindymindypindy.blog spot.com, and cindymindypindy.etsy.com.

## JENNIFER KHOSHBIN

Jennifer Khoshbin studied at the University of Kentucky and University of Texas in Austin, Texas, and is currently working toward an MFA. She owns a busy shop in San Antonio, Texas, where she creates and sells her work.

Her art is often seen as a journey into nostalgia through the use of vintage books and paper cutting techniques embellished with a variety of drawings. Jennifer's work has been exhibited in numerous solo and group exhibitions including the Bellevue Arts Museum, UPPERCASE Gallery in Canada, and Tinlark Gallery in Los Angeles. See more of Jennifer's work at jenkhoshbin.com.

## NICOLE LOMBARDO

Nicole Lombardo spends many hours sitting in front of her computer designing scrolls and embellishments for scrapbooking and other paper arts. In addition to creating designs for her own business and an invitation company, Nicole designs die-cuts for magisticalmemories.com. She went to school for graphic design and has worked in the field for more than a decade. See more of Nicole's work at niklindesigns1225.etsy.com and niklin1225.blogspot.com.

## JANINE MAVES

Janine Maves is a professional artist who has studied all over the United States. She has a B.A. in art, and has worked as a graphic artist. She has been a silk painter for more than 20 years, but works in many different mediums including paper art, jewelry, and unique hand-painted accessories. She is a member of Silk Painters International, Surface Design Association, Worldwide Women Artists Online (WWAO), Boomers, Freethinkers,

Trunkt, and Interior Design Teams. See more of Janine's work at altheaperegrine.com and onedogtalking.etsy.com.

## TINA TARNOFF

Tina Tarnoff was born in Zagreb, Croatia, in 1974. After careening through her childhood and teenage years, she left Zagreb at the age of 18 and embarked on the path of liberation. That path took her to London, where she dived into a vivacious city, developed the skills needed for survival, and learned cultural tolerance and appreciation. The road curved and twirled and continued around the world. After returning to her homeland, Tina started writing poetry and was published in various literary magazines. Tina now lives in San Francisco and works in a variety of mediums and styles, from oil painting and charcoal drawing to portraiture and paper cut art. See more of Tina's work at tinatarnoff.etsy.com and terrytarnoff.com/tina.

## KATHLEEN TRENCHARD

A native of New Orleans and graduate of Pratt Institute in Brooklyn, New York, with a masters in painting and printmaking, Kathleen Trenchard maintains a studio near downtown San Antonio, Texas. She has been working in traditional Mexican papel picado (punched paper) ever since she was introduced to the technique while visiting Huixcolotla, near the city of Puebla, Mexico, in the early 1990s. Kathleen has participated in many solo and group exhibits while teaching at San Antonio and Palo Alto colleges. Her book, *Mexican Papercutting*, was published by Lark Books in 1998 and is available through the Internet. See more of Kathleen's work at cut-it-out.org.

## LA DONNA WELTER

La Donna Welter is a mixed-media artist. The majority of her work combines the arts of scherenschnitte, paper cutting, and paper sculpture. Each piece is hand cut from fine artist's paper. La Donna holds teaching degrees from the University of Northern Iowa and the University of Wisconsin-Whitewater. She grew up on a farm in Iowa, but now calls Keller, Texas, home. See more of La Donna's art at ladonnawelter.blogspot.com and lollishops.com/la-donna-papercuts. E-mails are welcome at welterladonna@aol.com.

# Index

**A**

Acorn Luminary 42

Adhesives 12

Alice Invents Book Sculpture 62

**B**

The Beetle's Devotion 78

Bird of Paradise Ikebana
    Pop-Up Card 90

Buckingham, Barbara 22, 70, 125

Butterfly Grave 80

**C**

Choi, Karin Marlett 42, 54, 56, 90, 125

Christian, Holly 24, 36, 102, 125

Cowgirl Apron 102

Cutting & Scoring 16

Cutting Tools 13

**D**

Dimensional Décor 40

Dolly 76

**E**

Eliminating Creases & Folds 17

Emerlye, Cynthia 38, 84, 125

**F**

Fairies in the Vines Ornament 60

Falling Leaves Window Valance 56

Feathered Friends Treat Cone 98

Ferguson, Cynthia 5, 26, 30, 32, 74,
    78, 92, 96, 98, 100, 126

Flowers & Butterfly Card 88

For Give and Take 82

Frames & Embellishments 94

The Frog Prince 100

**G**

Gate-Fold Invitation 22

Getting Started 10

Ginkgo Leaf Lampshade 54

**H**

Heron Ornament 46

**I**

Initial Gift Tag 92

**K**

Khoshbin, Jennifer 2, 62, 68, 80, 126

Kirigami Card 84

Kirigami Mandala 38

**L**

Large Flower Ornament 58

Let's Celebrate 20

Lombardo, Nicole 94, 126

**M**

Maves, Janine 46, 50, 58, 60, 126

Meet the Designers 125

Miniature Papel Picado Flag 34

Mounting & Framing Paper Cuts 17

**N**

Never-Too-Late Book Sculpture 68

**O**

Orange Street & Broad Street
    Gates 70

**P**

Paper 14

Paper Forest 50

Patterns 105

Preserving & Storing Paper Cuts 18

**S**

Squirrel in the Woods Card
    & Envelope 96

Suitable for Framing 64

The Swan 66

**T**

Tarnoff, Tina 66, 88, 127

Tassel Shelf Liner 48

Tea Apron 24

Tea Party Centerpiece 26

Tea Party Place Cards 30

Tea Party Placemat 32

Techniques 16

Tools & Materials 12

Trenchard, Kathleen 34, 48, 127

The Twins 74

**U**

Using Patterns 19

**W**

Welcome Spring Table Runner 36

Welter, La Donna 1, 76, 127